Holiday FLOWER ARRANGEMENTS

ARRANGEMENT FOR A HOLIDAY (Frontispicce): *This idea is suited to most holiday decoration. Fill a hurricane chimney, or any crystal-clear container, with cherries as in the picture, or with cranberries at Thanksgiving, with blown-glass tree balls at Christmas, with colored eggs at Easter, or with any seasonal material. Keep available greens fresh in a small bowl of water concealed by the filling to give an effect both novel and lovely. If container is not footed, an inverted glass bowl will supply an appropriate base. Candles can match or contrast in hue.*

ARRANGER: ANN HAGAN PHOTOGRAPHER: WILLIAM HOWLAND COURTESY: GOOD HOUSEKEEPING MAGAZINE

Holiday FLOWER ARRANGEMENTS

EDITED BY EMMA H. CYPHERS

Hearthside Press
INCORPORATED
Publishers • New York

Library of Congress Catalog Card Number 54-11631
Printed in the United States of America

Contents

Holiday FLOWER ARRANGEMENTS

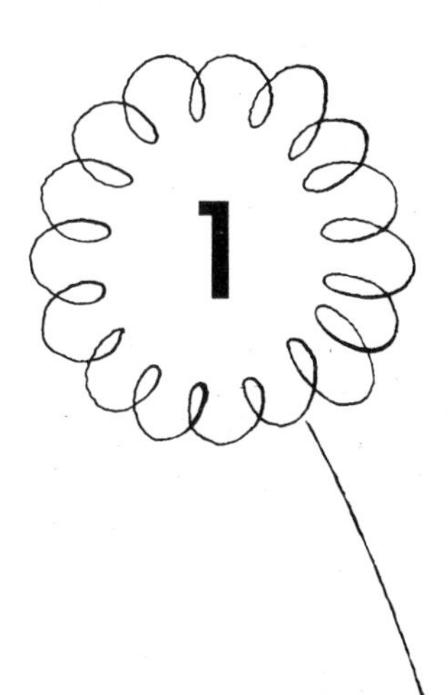

Decorative Flower Arrangements

MAKE THEM AS INDIVIDUAL AS A MONOGRAM

Whether your home is simple and casual, or formal and elegant, flower arrangements will add a graceful touch, a final and very personal one. Plant materials from your own garden or from the wayside, and occasionally from the florist, thoughtfully and lovingly arranged, will transfer your personality to your dwelling. Your selection and arrangements of flowers will individualize it as surely as does your monogram on fine linens and lingerie.

Flower arrangements satisfy a deep need for self-expression, for nothing else so requires the hands, eyes, mind, and heart to work in unison. Beautiful arrangements that express the thought and personality of the maker always catch the eye of anyone who enters a room, whether a member of the family, a friend, or a casual caller.

Flowers are an economical means of beautifying your home. They may be grown easily and inexpensively in your own garden or found abundantly in God's Green Acre, without a price tag, in spring, summer, or fall. And little or no money is required even when the unproductive winter months have depleted outside bloom, for it is possible to force barren branches from tree or shrub into flower or leafage within doors. Or you may use cuttings from well-grown house plants for fashioning attractive arrangements. Though the florist can furnish an abundance of flowers the year round, you will need only a handful of his blossoms for combining with other plant material.

The techniques for forcing, cutting, and conditioning to insure the longest possible life in plant materials, as well as drying for special purposes, are explained later in this book wherever they apply to specific decorations.

don't doubt your own ability

If lists of "dos and don'ts" have filled you with doubts as to your ability to combine flowers into beautiful and decorative designs, this is the book for you. So brief a text can present only suggestions for so vast a subject as flower arrangement, but I want chiefly to focus your attention on potentialities. The illustrations are selected with an eye to basic suggestion, to kindle within you a spark of imagination that will set your own thinking afire to produce your own outstanding designs.

The easiest way to decorate, of course, is to continue along an old familiar pattern or plan, or to copy the work of others. But in following the easy route, you will deny yourself much pleasure. To attempt something new and different requires thought, but in the process, your interest and pleasure will be greatly stimulated. I suggest that you plan new decorations for future occasions by studying the illustrations without intending or desiring to copy them. Consider thoughtfully your own reactions to the work of others, and make your personal conclusions about what you would do with the same or similar material.

Every person has an ego, an urge to excel. In flower arrangement, as in all things, this is so. It will be good for your ego to work toward better and different arrangements. Not only will such effort serve as an artistic outlet, but it will develop your perspective on everything in life—on yourself, on everyone with whom you come in contact, even on the inanimate things around you, and on every experience in your daily adventure of living. Seeing the possibility of beautiful designs around you will help you live more fully and, what is more significant, add richness to the lives of your family, your friends, and even the strangers who see your handiwork.

But in following your urge to excel, do not take flower arrangement too seriously. I do not mean to imply that a lovely floral design can be executed without thought and plan, for surface beauty in all things is more than skin-deep. All beauty is supported by an underlying structure. And so it is in flower arrangement—in the completed design and in its component parts of plant material, container, and accessories. But in any undertaking, Americans are apt to follow an extreme pattern that is the opposite to the intended relaxation. In decorating try to avoid this.

arrange flowers for pleasure

It is right that an arranger who is displaying work at a public flower show should strive for perfection. But in the home, the objective is quite different. In the home, a flower arrangement is but part of the pattern for producing a warm, cheerful, and friendly atmosphere. In the exhibition hall, the arrangement functions individually as an exacting subject composed within a limited and defined space.

The intent of this book, therefore, is to serve as encouragement to homemakers unschooled in flower show exhibiting. At the same time I hope that it will aid experienced exhibitors to forget that they must please the judge at all costs. First and foremost, be true to yourself! Arrange flowers for what pleasure there may be in it for you, and if you are working at home, for what charm they can add to your home. In short, plan what you personally would like to do, and carry that plan to completion in the manner of your choice.

This method will not excuse careless thinking or working, however. Home decoration need not be planned in minute detail, but the results should be something more than merely a bunch of flowers in a vase. A building up of harmony is the foundation of all enterprise in work or play. In flower arrangement, you need to know how to achieve suitability or "fitness," but use this knowledge as naturally as when it guides your choice and wearing of clothes.

harmonious relationship is not difficult

Too many floral groupings in a room will make it look as though ready for a public reception, just as overdressing can make a woman appear costumed for a masquerade. On the other hand, a judicious use of great masses of flowers can impart an exciting atmosphere for a gala occasion, even as "ribbons and bows" can give high spirits to the wearer. Flower decoration is the most adaptable single item of any room, so harmonious relationship is not a difficult quality to produce.

I suggest that you consider what you have accomplished so far in home decoration. Doubtless, your home furnishings and accessories have been purchased and placed with suitability to your living plan in mind—that is, fitness for their purpose, for your requirements, for placement, and for pleasing appearance, since you must live with them daily. As you look at them, you know whether you like their color, size, shape, texture, and position in the room. Simply transfer this daily experience of selecting or criticizing other objects in your home to the suitability of your flower arrangements. In designing them, consider such essential things as color, texture, size, shape, character, and placement.

As to color, the eye is the final judge. You may study color charts to improve your perception and sensibility. But your daily experiences in seeing and choosing it in home furnishings and dress should help you to determine what is or is not pleasing to you in the color plan of a flower arrangement.

Your knowledge of gratifying texture relationship also increases as life goes on. So, for general consideration, no special talent for understanding texture suitability in flower arrangement is required.

For size and shape harmony, at least in the ordinary problem, rely on your instinctive perception of proportion and on your commonsense attitude toward daily things that you have accepted or rejected without question.

set the scheme with a dominant idea

Even the character of a decorative plan is a matter of general understanding. No one is completely happy when uncertain or in doubt about something. Applying this to flower arrangement, it simply means that one dominant idea, thought, feeling, or substance should set the scheme for all else. For example, flowers and leaves of rugged growth are in character with materials that have similar casual qualities, such as the unfinished structural frame of a cabin in the woods. The design in such a relationship would be unassuming. On the other hand, in a formal setting, a container of classic lines and smooth texture, holding aristocrats of the flower kingdom, would be in proper relationship.

As to suitability of placement, consider the decorative purpose. Is the decoration to bring a bright and cheery spot to a dark or dreary corner? If so, select flowers in warm and sunny hues, and arrange them in a well-polished metal container. The shine and brilliance of such a combination gives an illusion of light and sparkle, and so is "fitting." Is the arrangement to be placed on the breakfast table in front of a sunny window to cheer the morning sleepyhead? If so, the form of plant material and the contour or silhouette of the completed design will have more appeal than color, for light shining through petals tends to deaden their hue. Will it be seen at eye level, on a mantel perhaps? If so, something to trail over might well be selected for a softening effect that makes it "fit." For the mantel, a very tall vase with long-stemmed flowers is not in accord with the location. Such a combination is more suitable for a low table or even for judicious placement on the floor.

In short, the suitability of the component parts of decoration and the location of the completed design must achieve together a harmonious unity, or oneness. You cannot attain even the slightest degree of your share of life's happiness if you do not have a harmonious relationship with your environment and with your fellow man. Be sure to use this idea of harmony and unity in your flower arrangements.

celebrating with flowers

Accenting some event close to the heart with the tokens of Nature has always had appeal. Literature and history recount the use of flowers and plant growth for celebrations and rewards throughout the ages of man. Decorative wreaths and garlands, festoons woven of flowers, fruit, and leaves are recorded since before the birth of Christ. Ancient Romans spent fabulous sums for roses, the petals of which were used to cover the reclining couches of family and friends at festive banquet tables. The Greeks crowned the winners at the Pythian games with wreaths of laurel, and such wreaths were also given for academic honors.

Decoration with plant material, therefore, has an imperishable heritage. To help you carry on this beautiful tradition of celebration and honor, here is this book of suggestions—*Holiday Flower Arrangements.*

1 THANKSGIVING ELEGANCE: *Grapes, in hues ranging from green to russet to russet-violet, are arranged in beautiful black marble urns with bronze bas-relief on their pedestals. At the base large "black" grapes, broccoli heads, and a dark green grooved acorn squash add weight and texture. Ivy in tones of green present rhythmic line. The flat wooden base is dark, grayed blue-violet. An air of dignity is achieved through the elevation of one urn upon a dull black block of wood.*

ARRANGER: MRS. RAYMOND R. STOLTZ PHOTOGRAPHER: BOUTRELLE

Thanksgiving

USE SYMBOLS
OF PLENTY AND HARVEST COLORS

As a family day, typically American in tradition, Thanksgiving is enjoyed in the same spirit and with the same symbols of plenty as in the time of the Pilgrims at Plymouth. Decorations are gracious and colorful, for Nature gives us the largess of garden, vineyard, and field at what is possibly the peak in variety of plant material. The seasons' gifts attest that through time's endless cycle God's plan is manifest. Summer days have fulfilled the promise of spring with golden grains, plump and luscious grapes, fragrant ruddy apples, large moonfaced pumpkins, and other fruits and vegetables in variety.

The harvest clearly emphasizes that order is an underlying principle of life. The tiniest of plants grow and flourish, producing colorful foliage and flowers to give aesthetic pleasure. All nature works toward bearing fruit or seed that will miraculously continue life. Nature's never-ending cycle is thus declared, and man recognizes in it his need for order—in short, the art of planning or design.

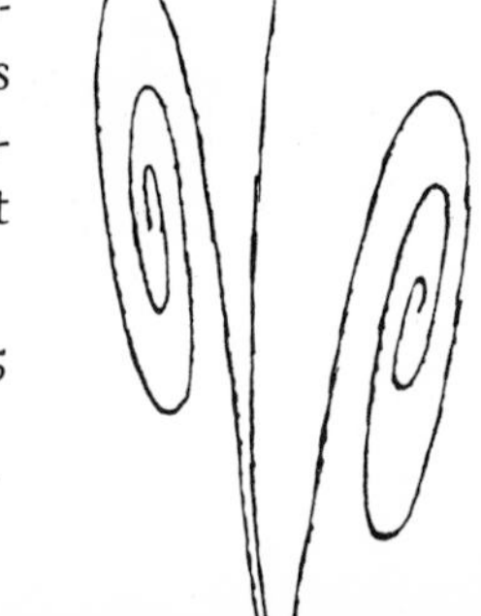

2 BOLD AND STURDY: *In an antique lamp base, Scotch broom and English laurel, gray-green euphorbia, and tan wheat make a beautiful silhouette. Gladiolus, dahlias, and chrysanthemums range in hue from yellow through copper to rust. "Black" grapes, apples, small pears, peppers, green bananas, and osage oranges repeat the colors of the ceramic pheasant.*

ARRANGER: MRS. GEORGE J. HIRSCH PHOTOGRAPHER: HERBERT STUDIOS

November plant materials
(plates 1, 2, 3, 4, 6, 7, 10, 13)

In addition to edible fruits for your arrangements, you will find branches bright with colorful berries in interesting growth patterns, and branches in intriguing shapes though bare of summer foliage. You will find seed pods in fascinating design, interesting grasses, and golden Indian maize. There are flowers, too, for the garden is rich with chrysanthemums.

flowers of the harvest season
(plates 2, 4, 7)

Flowers either alone or in combination are fitting to dress the mantel or occasional table in the living room or entrance hallway. For the flowers of fall—chrysanthemums—there is no lovelier container than the cornucopia of heavy glass or pottery in an upright position. With garden bloom at a premium in many sections of the country at Thanksgiving time, this "flower of the month" is coveted for its decorative appeal.

Bright and dark colored bloom, running the gamut from red and orange to rust and maroon, looks particularly happy with berried branches and strong dark foliage for height and accent. Containers of wood or pottery in earthy tones, perhaps drab for the lighter hues, acquire an amazing glamour when they serve as frames for these colorful flowers. Intriguing shapes in driftwood or heavy bare branches in rhythmic patterns are suited in character to the "raggedy" mums. But chrysanthemums vary so much in texture that you should have as good a selection in your garden as you have of fruits and vegetables in your larder. Just as there are comparatively coarse or refined examples in the latter—such as hooked-neck squash and potatoes for contrast with smooth peppers, silver-skinned onions, or fragile white grapes—so there are among chrysanthemums the little elegant pompons and the large and heavy flowers, the compact forms and the feathery and loose-petaled varieties.

All through the year, you will experience the greatest pleasure in your decorative arrangements by emphasizing the seasonal charac-

teristics. In your design patterns, place the emphasis on the distinctive qualities of the plant material that is available at each season, on the special beauty that distinguishes flowers, berries, fruit, foliage, seed pods, or shapely branches, as one season follows another in Nature's plan.

inspiration in symbolism
(plates 1, 7, 17)

Plant material has always held symbolism for man. Especially at this season, you will find inspiration in the spiritual associations of fruits, vegetables, grains, foliage, and flowers. Among the lavish gifts of the season, grapes stand for the blood of life, and figs for life itself. Ivy is for friendship and good cheer, and pineapple is synonymous with hospitality. The lowly corn symbolizes wealth. And who

3 (Left) WARMTH IN HARVEST DECORATION: *Against a gray pickled-oak wall, a basket-shaped piece of weathered wood on a dark brown plank holds branches, gourds, and hickory nuts in opened shells. Rooster, hen, and chick, hand made from wheat straw, add character and distinction.*

ARRANGER: MRS. RHYNOLD G. SCHULKE PHOTOGRAPHER: THE NILES DAILY TIMES

4 (Below) REFRESHING DESIGN: *In an unusually pleasing study, bleached wheat, yellow chrysanthemums, bronzy-red peony foliage, mountain spinach pods in tones of brown and beige, and red and green grapes, are combined in a hand-made wooden goblet on a hand-rubbed plaque, both of walnut.*

ARRANGER: MRS. JOHN W. KNIGHT, JR. PHOTOGRAPHER: DWITE WALKER

among us is not rich with blessings? It seems fitting to show gratitude even in so small a matter as plant selection based on the symbolism of the ages.

make use of harvest color
(plates 1, 2, 7, 8, 10, 12)

In November, more than at any other time, you can enjoy to the full in your arrangements the fiery hues of autumn tempered by the somber purples of grapes and eggplant and the brown tones of nuts and dried grasses or grains. Plan to carry some of the color and splendor of the harvest into your design. Here you can test your selective ability, for the profusion of material may tempt you to mix too many hues or combine too many forms in a single composition.

suitable containers

Compotes or tureens are useful containers, and epergnes are equally effective. If a degree of formality is desired, a classic urn, as in Plate 1, holds the harvest bounty with special grace.

For a casual effect, containers ingeniously made from natural forms are interesting (Plates 3, 6, 7). Scooped-out pumpkins (Plate 7), eggplants, squashes, or giant gourds, work beautifully into a definite color plan. To use the fruits of the season in this manner, select those that will stand securely in proper position. Cut or saw off the top, and scoop out the seeds. Gourds will last indefinitely if they have been allowed to dry thoroughly for three or four weeks and then given a protective coating of wax. An inserted bowl of water will keep flowers fresh, as a pretty complement to fruit and vegetable groupings.

appropriate bases
(plates 1, 6, 12, 13, 14, 16)

Bases (stands, blocks, plaques) are as important as containers. When they relate in hue and texture they add distinction to any composition. It is often desirable to apply a coat of paint to harmonize with a chosen base. A mat finish paint is generally more attractive than a shiny one for sheen pulls the eye to such a degree that it becomes a dominant force in the design. Like a container, a base is but a *part—*

5 FALL BOUNTY IN GREEN, WHITE, AND BLACK: *A black metal cart planter is a unique container for white chrysanthemums, glossy green ivy leaves, fuzzy green teasel gourds, other gourds in green and white, variegated euonymous, and black sugar-cane seed heads.*

ARRANGER: MRS. LOUIS H. AMER PHOTOGRAPHER: CARPENTER'S STUDIO

important in its role but subordinate to the plant material used with it. A water paint which dries to a dull texture is practical, for it can be easily washed away when its hue is no longer desired. In using a base painted with such a finish, be careful not to splash the surface with water or unsightly spots will result.

6 THE HARVEST EXPRESSED WITH SIMPLICITY: *If you prefer restraint of line to mass, here is a charming example for November. Apple tree branches, green squash, brown seed pods, light gray-green field mullein, limes, and chartreuse osage oranges in a bracket fungus container are arranged on a brown oval plank. Textures are particularly noteworthy: crinkly, wooly, ribbed, and smooth, with rough predominating.*
ARRANGER: MRS. GERSON T. HIRSCH PHOTOGRAPHER: BOUTRELLE

7 IN A PUMPKIN SHELL: *A bowl of water inserted in a hollowed pumpkin shell keeps plant material fresh. Combined here are beige-toned dried corn tassels and leaves, garnet-red sumac seed cones, mahogany-red canna foliage, three varieties of chrysanthemums in rust touched with yellow, and colorful dried Indian corn.*

ARRANGER: MRS. EDWIN B. DEAN PHOTOGRAPHER: BOUTRELLE

dominance and contrast
(plates 2, 6, 11, 15)

In designing your arrangement, simply apply the common-sense principles of order to the art of arranging. One shape, one hue, one texture must dominate and thereby set the theme. Then it is well to introduce a contrast, for variety lends spice in art as it does in life. This contrast or opposition can be one of shape, line, hue, or texture to break the monotony of the dominant pattern. By being different, it will call attention to and thereby emphasize the importance of the dominant character. But only an accent of opposition is required. Kept subordinate, it will enrich and beautify your arrangement.

the harvest dining table
(plates 14, 15, 16, 17)

Enjoyment of the Thanksgiving meal is increased tenfold if the festive setting presents the "fruits of the earth" to symbolize a life overflowing with goodness and beauty. Group large, medium, and small sizes, contrasting in form and harmonious hues, in a rhythmic sweep from high to low in a container as in Plate 12. Or let them spill from a woven reed cornucopia—the horn of plenty, itself a symbol of abundance—onto a suitable base. Fruits and vegetables, alone or combined, are effective arranged without a container on a tray or platter, or on a wooden plaque. For practical reasons, they should never be arranged directly on the table or cloth. Plate 16 illustrates foliage, washed free of dust and spray, as an appropriate "base".

how to secure fruit in arrangements
(plates 10, 16, 17)

To keep rounded forms in place on a flat base, impale one comparatively large fruit or vegetable on a needle pin holder. As a harmonious design is built up around this structural beginning, secure the other fruit with plastic toothpicks thrust into neighboring material. Fruits arranged to fall over the rim are attractive and the effect is worth the little trouble it takes to securely wire bunches of grapes, one at each end, to a lightweight branch placed across the opening. A thin wooden dowel stick will also serve this purpose. This support is concealed when other fruits are added.

If high placement is desired, fruits can be impaled on tips of branches or ends of wooden sticks cut to desired lengths, and these "stems" concealed in the body of the design (Plate 3).

In a grouping as illustrated in Plates 2 and 10, crushed chicken wire in the container will give sufficient body and shape so that less fruit

8 AN ATMOSPHERE OF HOSPITALITY: *Against a green wall, the analogous hues and values of yellow, orange, red-orange, and red are effective. Chrysanthemums predominate, but palm spray, sea oats, oak leaves, strawberry corn, pumpkin, the chartreuse tray, and the wine bottle lend line, form, texture, and story interest.*
ARRANGER: MRS. GEORGE GOLDSON PHOTOGRAPHER: BOUTRELLE

is required to build up the finished picture. Economy is always welcome where decoration is focused on food, as at Thanksgiving.

Foliage, such as grape leaves or short lengths of vine, kept fresh in small vials of water inserted at strategic spots between the fruits and vegetables, lighten any tendency toward heaviness when forms are closely grouped in a mass effect. (Plates 1, 10).

9 TRIBUTE TO THE ORIGINAL CAST: *Designed for a party, the black Pilgrim's hat is a fitting companion for an old Bible opened to "A Song of Thanksgiving". White chrysanthemums and pine arranged in an elongated-S line (Hogarth's Line of Beauty) frame the hat and carry the eye to the Bible, thereby combining three unrelated units into one well-harmonized composition.*
ARRANGER: MRS. RAYMOND R. STOLTZ PHOTOGRAPHER: BOUTRELLE

10 PEACE AND PLENTY: *Yellow-green squash, green and red peppers, pears, yellow apples, crab apples, red and purple grapes, and ivy are arranged in a distinctive container, a French egg basket. While this arrangement was designed as an entry in a flower show, it would be striking at home on the sideboard, or as decoration on a green cloth for a buffet setting.*
ARRANGER: MRS. JAMES L. FINCH PHOTOGRAPHER: BOUTRELLE

11 IN THE SPIRIT OF THE DAY: *On dining-room buffet, or on side or dining table (where its height will not interfere with those seated), this charming decoration reflects distinctive taste. Green ivy and magnolia leaves, zucchini squash, and peppers contrast in hue with red scales. For transition between these contrasting hues, red in the container, green in the plant material, red peppers are included in the vegetable grouping. Cauliflower, endive, and white onions add highlights.*

ARRANGER: MRS. ROBERT STRAUB PHOTOGRAPHER: BOUTRELLE

treating and preserving plant materials
(plates 6, 14)

It is imperative to give special treatment to some plant materials to insure lasting qualities. Plate 6 illustrates wooly-textured gray field mullein which requires special attention to "harden" it. Take up the rosette by the roots and completely immerse in water for an hour or so before combining it with other materials in arrangement. Give the clump an occasional deep soaking and it will remain fresh and crisp for an amazingly long time, to be used again and again in decoration.

Various tree branches retain their leaves almost indefinitely if they are kept in a solution of one-third glycerine and two-thirds water. Peel the bark as you would any woody branch for better water absorption and soak in several inches of the prepared solution. Water evaporates, so if the branches are to be used over a long period of time, add more water from time to time; glycerine need not be replenished. Many varieties can be so preserved; half the fun is in experimenting to discover those you find most beautiful and satisfying.

12 CASUAL CHARM: A *delightful table piece in tones of gold, brown, yellow, green, orange and purple. Dried materials (wheat, okra, and jacaranda pods) give height to fruits and vegetables grouped in an old wooden butter bowl on a woven straw mat base. Although orderly, the design appears carefree and spontaneous, the touch of an artist. The spectator's eye is effortlessly carried through the rhythmic composition.*

ARRANGER: MRS. F. PALMER HART PHOTOGRAPHER: BOUTRELLE

13 (Above) FANCY FREE AND WHIMSICAL: *A mood of delightful intimacy is apparent in this grouping of green and yellow gourds, dried corn tassels, and autumn-tinted oak leaves on a bamboo base. It denotes a spirit of fun and is appropriate to Halloween as well as to Thanksgiving.*
ARRANGER: MRS. LOUIS H. AMER PHOTOGRAPHER: EDWARD NAHER

14 (Right) WHEN THE COCK CROWS: *This clever work would be fine for a Thanksgiving breakfast table, silhouetted against strong light at a sunny window. A terra cotta bowl on its own brown base holds natural and red-brown sea oats, beige and green okra pods, glycerine-treated copper beech. The beige rooster repeats the okra green on his head and around his feet. A hand-finished redwood plaque rests on a coarse green cloth.*
ARRANGER: MRS. JOHN W. KNIGHT, JR. PHOTOGRAPHER: DWITE A. WALKER

try other Thanksgiving arrangements

Why not symbolize the good cheer that will be in your home at Thanksgiving time by designing an arrangement for your entrance door? Tie a grouping of Indian corn and oak branches to the knocker with weatherproof ribbon in harmonizing hues.

Make a charm string by tying fruits, vegetables, and seed pods, with raffia, to a stout rope suitable for hanging on a wall space that needs a gay fall atmosphere. A long dried okra stalk with pods, hung upside down, is a good foundation in place of rope.

Or thin out the tops of pineapples, insert tall slender candles, and place these homemade holders on a clean fan-shaped palm leaf. Make your own arrangement of small fruits and nuts at the base.

Make use of the pods of hollyhock, lunaria, laburnum, or locust. Their silvery cast adds textural interest to fruit and vegetable arrangements.

The harvest is at its best. The illustrations we have selected and suggested show it is possible to give an impression of bounteous splendor in a wide range of designs. Thanksgiving decoration can be delicate, sophisticated, even bold; there is a style compatible with the décor of any home.

AN ARRANGEMENT FOR SENTIMENTAL OCCASIONS (facing page 32): *Ranging from open bloom to buds, Red Favorite roses in an informal glass pitcher are arranged in a simple triangular pattern.*
ARRANGER: MYRA BROOKS PHOTOGRAPHER: ROCHE COURTESY: FLOWER GROWER

15 FOR THE HARVEST BUFFET: *A nostalgic mood is created by an old red and white tablecloth, white ironstone plates, and red hobnail glasses, combined with grapes, peppers, artichokes, tomatoes, crab apples, wheat and ivy on a "lazy Susan" of natural wood. Textured napkins are white. A thick candle rather than a hand-dipped taper is a wise choice to add height and balance the weight of the grouping.*
ARRANGER: MRS. JAMES L. FINCH PHOTOGRAPHER: BOUTRELLE

16 TABLE FOR A FAMILY DINNER: *Damask cloth and green napkins emphasize the amethyst of stemware, patterned plates, and fruit. Other colors in the plate are repeated in a pair of ceramic pheasants set amidst the fruit on a base of glossy magnolia leaves. The decoration is well-proportioned to the size of the table and harmonious in shape repetition, two important considerations for pleasing effect.*

ARRANGER: MRS. JOHN M. LANGENBERGER PHOTOGRAPHER: ROCHE

17 A FLOWER-SHOW TABLE OF ELEGANCE: *Inspiration for an elaborate home table, this publicly-exhibited setting features an exquisite convent linen cloth embroidered with gold thread, dark green, gold-banded china, Steuben glasses, and gold-based hurricane candlesticks with an arrangement of symbolic harvest fruits. Pineapples and some of the artichokes are delicately sprayed with gold, other artichokes in natural green, limes, and magnolia foliage complete a stunning grouping on a gold-tooled Italian tray.*

ARRANGER: MRS. RHYNOLD G. SCHULKE PHOTOGRAPHER: CLEVELAND PRESS

Christmas

COMBINE THE SPIRITUAL QUALITIES WITH GAIETY AND JOY

If arrangements were rated by universality of appeal, those planned for the Yuletide would surely win top honor. We expect to find in them something besides a pattern of color and form, for even though we plan to make the season merry, we look for an expression of the spiritual beauty of the Christmas story, a story as unchangeable and as immortal as mother love. The last month of the year, therefore, brings you a challenge in decorating.

It is a gracious privilege, in the sanctity of your home, to offer Nature's flora in tribute to the Prince of Peace, born in a lowly stable almost two thousand years ago. There was no preparation for his coming then, but today Christians everywhere—in lonely outposts, in crowded cities, in all temperatures and climes—make ready wholeheartedly for the holy day that commemorates the birth of Jesus.

18 FOR THE FRONT DOOR: *Concentric circles of cones, pods, and cedar in tones of green, chartreuse, and brown, fringed with a ruffle of copper screening, the whole trimmed with dull moss-green and brown grosgrain ribbon, make a "corsage of charm".*
ARRANGER: MRS. H. G. STATON
PHOTOGRAPHER: JEANETTE GROSSMAN

19 ADVENT WREATH: *Advent is a four-week period of preparation for Christmas, just as Lent is preparation for Easter. It is fun to trim a wreath with appropriate symbols as the days move along. Here added to one of fir are old-fashioned paper toys, little stuffed animals, bells, stars, and various tree ornaments. Children particularly enjoy this type of decoration for as symbols are added through the weeks, stimulation is kept at high pitch.*
ARRANGER: MRS. H. G. STATON
PHOTOGRAPHER: JEANETTE GROSSMAN

20 CHRISTMAS MESSAGE ON THE DOOR: *Everyone loves jolly fat Santa and here, waving a cheery greeting, he is an amusing addition to this fondly-contrived doorway decoration. A candle stub fastened securely on the point of a nail hammered from the bottom through the floor of a wicker hanging plant basket suggests the familiar sentiment "to light the way". The rustic, rigid post from which the "lantern" hangs is softened with greens whitened with plastic "snow".*

ARRANGER: MRS. JACK R. CAMPBELL PHOTOGRAPHER: ROCHE

Christmas colors, bright and sparkling
(plates 19, 23, 24, 25, 26, 30, 34, 41)

Home is the best-loved place in the world. Especially at Christmas, it is a magnet drawing even wanderers to its hearth. When you decorate, do it gaily. Color can sing and sparkle without reservation, for the world wears such shining armor for a brief span only. But in the wearing, it inspires expectation of the wonderful to happen, as indeed it does. Grim tension breaks, and all humanity is pulled closely together to share in a spirit of love, warmth, and brightness—for this is Christmas.

The popular hues of December reveal in symbolism the inner meaning of Christmas. Green, for example, stands for everlasting life, and red for joy and laughter. Blue speaks of quiet, spiritual calm, and white, of purity. Through all, silver and gold shine with the radiance of the Christ Child's birthday.

When gilding greens, use paint sparingly. Allow some green to show through for the most beautiful effect. A softer, less metallic luster results if more powder is mixed with the thinning liquid than the directions of the gilding preparation suggest. A bit of antique bronze powder or brown paint added to the mixture supplies richness and elegance.

traditional plant materials

Anew each year is the old truth, "Christmas is what you make it." One of the joys it brings is the anticipation, the "getting ready." But there is no need for elaborate trimmings. Abiding charm lies in traditional materials that are easily available. With imagination and ingenuity, the old familiar things can be combined in design so different in appeal that they appear to be almost new. Among many things, clippings from the yard, pine cones, acorns, dried seed pods can yield a welcome return in their subdued natural appearance or gilded for unusual luster. If you purchase holly and other traditional greens, be sure that they are nursery-grown for decorative purposes, not cut ruthlessly for sale on city streets.

Poinsettias require special treatment to prevent immediate wilting when their stems are cut. Sear the cut end with flame until it is well charred and the milky sap stops running from the stalk. Place the seared stem in deep cool water for at least several hours, preferably overnight, before arranging it alone or with other plant material for Christmas decoration. After the soaking period you may cut the stem to any desired length.

plan a doorway decoration

(plates 18, 19, 20)

The entrance sets the pattern of adornment throughout the home. Decorations may be dignified or mirth-provoking, usually depending on whether there are children in the home. Youngsters love a snow man extending rollicking welcome at the door, and if glistening snow makes a "white Christmas," the snow man seems at ease. His body is easily made of sacks stuffed with newspapers and covered with cotton batting. His eyes are cranberries; his nose, a small red apple. With a flat board in his hands for the birds' Christmas smörgasbord of suet, seeds, and crumbs, the snow man has great appeal.

The doorway itself is a symbol of hospitality decked with diversified materials. If the design is kept free of confusing detail, its charm can be appreciated from a distance and serve as a greeting to each passer-by.

Ingenuity is always the best ingredient. A red door carried one of the loveliest entrance decorations that I have ever seen. A tree designed

21 TRADITIONAL BEAUTY ON THE MANTEL: *Here festoons echo the ornamentation of a traditional room with no overdressing to cheapen the effect. The rope is of fine-leaved chamaecyparis, yew, and ivy which adds interesting shape and texture contrast. In the arrangement, yew and holly, with clumps of Jack-in-the-pulpit berries, are highlighted with gilded berries and fern spore cases.*
ARRANGER: MRS. K. D. SMITH PHOTOGRAPHER: ROCHE

in pleasing proportion and whitened with one of the imitation snow preparations was tied to a heavy brass knocker. Light bulbs concealed in shrubs at each side of the brick steps cast a soft glow at night, giving the tree a fragile, delicate appearance.

Such a tree is easy to do. As the foundation, use open-mesh wire screening and cut it with tin shears into a flat pyramidal tree shape. Wire it securely to a board foundation. Thrust short four-inch sprigs of green, stem end down, into the wire openings. For fullness, overlap the clippings as they are added from the top to the base. Finally, shape the tree by trimming off any pieces that spoil the contour. In its natural green or sprayed with paint, it is ready to be placed flush against the door.

You may hang on the door a decoration as traditional and simple as a wreath of evergreens, or as new as the triangular shape that symbolizes the Trinity. The inner edge, circular in contour, produces the "endless circle" to symbolize eternity. If the door is very plain, it can hold an unusual and fascinating treatment of three wreaths graduating in size from a large one near the bottom to a smaller one near the top.

how to make garlands, festoons, and roping
(plates 19, 21, 22, 23)

To make a plain green garland (wreath), lay a bunch of evergreen clippings, cut nine to ten inches in length, along a stiff wire hoop made firm by weaving around it long supple branches (as forsythia or willow). Wind a few turns of wire around this layer. Then add a second layer of greens overlapping the first enough to hide the wired end. Proceed in this manner around the frame until it is entirely covered with greens. Be sure that the wreath is well-filled yet not too thick, or the hole will be concealed. Cut off any extending ends that spoil the symmetry of the wreath.

22 SYMMETRY FOR FORMAL DIGNITY: A *well-proportioned festoon neatly hung above the fireplace, and a simple compact unit on the mantel, make the always-featured spot in the home even more so on Christmas.*
ARRANGER: MRS. JACK R. CAMPBELL PHOTOGRAPHER: ROCHE

23 WREATH FOR DINING TABLE OR WALL: *Glossy magnolia leaves are neatly stapled on a plywood ring foundation. Against this green, goodies (animal cookies, dried fruits, candied pineapple rings, cocktail tidbits, glued into groups with Dupont cement) are applied in three beautifully-proportioned accents. Leaves cut from copper and aluminum foil are added to this colorful and striking decoration.*

ARRANGER: MRS. H. G. STATON PHOTOGRAPHER: PORTLAND OREGONIAN

Fir, yew, juniper, and cedar are suitable greens for wreath making since they last well out of water. Spruce and hemlock are satisfactory materials for outside use if the climate is cold. Avoid them for indoor decoration as needles drop too quickly when the greens are not in water.

Ropings are made in much the same manner as a wreath except that the foundation is a stout rope. For a festoon (swag) make a foundation of plywood board cut to size and shape desired, covered with open-mesh wire screening, or wrapped with strips of cloth to make pockets into which the sprigs are inserted.

Wreaths and swags made of garden ivy or glossy magnolia leaves stapled on a plywood frame are magnificent (Plate 23). To prevent curling of the leaves when they are thus used without water, shellac the under side of each leaf before assembling the decoration.

The swag in Plate 22 is made with dried magnolia leaves, cones, and nuts wired to a plywood frame. Do not cut the foundation too wide or the finished decoration will be awkward and heavy in appearance.

A dried design such as this is a practical solution to busy day decoration for it can be constructed well in advance of the season. Cones can be gathered at any time throughout the year and magnolia leaves can be dried without special treatment. The completed decoration can be saved from year to year if it is carefully protected from dust between seasons. Until nuts are thoroughly dry, put moth preventive crystals in the storage box to discourage weevils.

The wreath in Plate 40 is easy to make. Choose materials in pleasing scale relationship to supply a variety of texture as in the combination of feathery juniper, smooth-leaved boxwood, and rose-hued California pepper berries shown in the illustration. Arrange clippings into

24 RED AND BRIGHT AS A HOLLY BERRY: *A buffet setting that is colorful, quick, and easy to do—a favored kind during the rush days of December. The key color, Christmas red of the cloth, is picked up in the old farmhouse design on dishes and coffee pot. Green bowl, napkins, and candles contrast in hue. Gray-green desert juniper with its large grayish berries is a transitional color between candle and cloth. Since this plant material lasts well without water, and will not stain the cloth, no container is needed.*

ARRANGER: MRS. JOHN M. LANGENBERGER PHOTOGRAPHER: DORRIS

25 THE NIGHT BEFORE CHRISTMAS: *". . . and all through the house, not a creature was stirring, not even a mouse. The stockings were hung by the chimney with care, in hopes that St. Nicholas soon would be there."* This *quotation from Clement Moore's "A Visit From St. Nicholas", is appealingly portrayed in an original composition. One's eyes move easily from the white Parian cat sleeping on his red felt pillow, through clustered red holly berries, variegated Oregon holly, and umbrella pine to the suggested mantel of white-painted wood molding, through the socks and back to the cat, tracing a well unified design.*

ARRANGER: MRS. LEONARD M. MATTHEWS
PHOTOGRAPHER: BOUTRELLE

a sufficient number of groupings to completely cover the dark green plastic frame purchased at little cost from the florist. The end of a two- to three-inch piece of pipe cleaner is wrapped around the stem ends of each grouping, the other end inserted into the styrofoam base. This easily and securely anchors the plant material. If the wreath will be seen from the back, cover it in like manner.

Inspired by the enameled ceramic work of the Italian Renaissance, a garland or festoon trimmed in the manner of Andrea Della Robbia —most famous member of a fifteenth century family of artists—never loses charm. Such a wreath, accented with fruit and cones and wound with ribbon, is as good today as it has been through the years.

wiring fruits, cones, and nuts

Wiring forms neatly and inconspicuously on to the wreath or festoon is easy once you acquire the knack. To secure cones, wind the wire around the lower sections, twisting it several times so that it is securely fastened. Leave a six- to eight-inch end to wind firmly around the frame.

To secure nuts, bore a hole through them, using a red hot needle held with a padding to protect you from burns. Pull a wire through the nut, twisting it tightly, and fasten the nut in place.

Round forms of fruits are easily managed. Push wires through the centers, twisting them together behind the fruits so that the wire is concealed when the fruit is on the frame. Impale small fruits such as cranberries or crab apples on toothpick "stems." Group them in bunches, then wire into place. To keep bunches of grapes in place, use hairpin-shaped wires, one at the stem end and one near the bottom of each bunch, pushed into the greens. Avoid pears, for as a rule their soft meat ripens too quickly.

If Della Robbia type decoration is planned for outdoor use, cover the fruit with two coats of shellac (after wiring and before securing them to the foundation) to prevent shriveling in freezing weather.

carry your door theme inside

If you have planned an interesting doorway decoration, a pleasing effect is gained by carrying the theme inside, thereby achieving a desired unity. Tying together all decoration with a story-telling idea or theme—"A White Christmas" for example—will inspire your design plan and result in that desired quality of oneness. (Plates 29, 42, 43). There is little satisfaction, little beauty for that matter, in decoration that offers nothing but a sprig of green above every picture and mirror, behind each wall light bracket, and spread to completely cover the mantel shelf.

theme possibilities

Several theme possibilities are suggested in the illustrations. There is, for example, "The Night Before Christmas," Plates 25, 31, and 32. Variations on a woodland theme are suggested in Plates 44, 45, and 46.

Plan a special interest spot in each important area in the room, and tie it in with the theme you have selected. In the living room one major climax, usually at the mantel, is enough with one or two lesser decorative units elsewhere in the room. From the living room the theme spreads throughout the house. For example, let us suppose the mood set is frivolous and gay as in Plate 41. Carry it up the stairway with greens and shiny tree balls suspended from under a simple handrail to terminate at the newel post with a concentrated grouping.

mantel designs
(plates 21, 22, 23)

Above the mantel, a festoon of evergreen clippings, such as juniper, fir or andromeda, brightened with bunches of cranberries, bayberries, rose hips, cones, or lunaria pods rubbed free of their outer covering, serves as a magnet of splendor. A very plain green roping accented only at those points where the ends of the festoon hang from a sagging crosspiece is lovely against a soft green wall.

26 CHRISTMAS YULE LOG: *Although the "log" has not been dragged from the woods to a manor hall as of old, this modern version of an ancient rite is appropriate on the mantel in today's living room. The natural wild cherry log in shades of brown rests on a heavy oak plaque. White pine, red and gold tree balls, and red satin bow are full of promise for a merry holiday, just as was that old time yule log kept burning during the twelve days of Christmas.*
ARRANGER: MRS. LOUIS H. AMER PHOTOGRAPHER: CARPENTER'S STUDIO

27 TRADITION AND CHARM IN THE HALL: *A modern version of the ancient kissing ball which in Merrie England hung from its own special hook, was the center of Christmas celebration long before the tree was used. To make it, use three circlets (embroidery hoops are excellent). Wrap each with satin ribbon (or evergreens) and slip one inside the other. Tie together at the intersections with ribbon and at the bottom cluster a sprig of mistletoe heavily laden with berries of course! This kissing ball is gold-wrapped to harmonize with the golden arborvitae. Clusters of green blown-glass balls, wired together, add gleam.*

ARRANGER: MRS. WILLIAM G. WHEELER PHOTOGRAPHER: BOUTRELLE

Gather berries in early fall before October rains spoil them. Remove all leaves, and hang the branches to dry in an airy place. Those with a semi-hard center, as rose hips, will last out of water an amazingly long time if brushed thoroughly with a solution of .50 per cent clear shellac and .50 per cent alcohol.

A swag of tarlatan or sateen caught up between two points, one high, one low, with blown glass tree balls or scrolls cut from aluminum alloy, makes a dramatic decoration over a mantel.

Against mellow wood paneling, a wreath or swag made entirely of various types and sizes of pine cones lightly touched with gold paint is exquisite in the color unity of gold and brown.

trees and trimming

The high spot of décor in many homes is the Christmas tree, and rightly so, for whether it is large or small, sentimental with nostalgic ornaments, or trimmed with special emphasis on one color, a Christmas tree is full of wonder. A floor-to-ceiling tree, trimmed with ornaments loved and saved through the years, is still a favorite, but traditional as most families are about Christmas, lack of space often requires a smaller size. Here is opportunity for unusual and distinctive trimming not practical on a large tree.

If your family has not enjoyed one dressed entirely with glass prisms or artificial icicles, they have missed much that is beautiful. The glass catches the light, breaking it into a carnival of color to reflect on the wall, a joy to behold.

Or a small tree hung with little white velvet or silver tinsel ribbon bows, or harboring a galaxy of birds with spunglass tails in its branches, suggests that "new" touch that designates the clever decorator. The important thing is not to sacrifice emotional richness for garish ornamentation.

A tree can be made at home with branches in a bowl. Cut two or three sprays in the length desired for the height of your tree. Fasten these together about four inches from the top with fine wire, and impale them on a needle pin holder in the bowl. Shape the tree with shorter pieces, using wire to hold sprays together. Short pieces at the base give form and help to hold the tree firmly in the bowl. Fill the container with water to keep the tree fresh throughout the Christmas season.

28 FOR AN OCCASIONAL TABLE: *Invested with the spirit of Christmas charm, this arrangement in an antique container is suited to many places in the home. Scotch broom sets the pattern, with lady apples, a profusion of crimson holly berries, and Oregon variegated holly forming the body of the design. A rare variety of holly matched in hue to the yellow side of the apples, seems to illuminate and add distinction. Dark green, shiny-leaved English holly serves as transition from the heart of the pattern to the extremities.*

ARRANGER: MRS. E. R. VAN LIEW PHOTOGRAPHER: CHARLES F. CYPHERS

table decorations

(plates 23, 24)

Dining tables, too, are specially decorated on Christmas day. An amusing breakfast setting with jolly old Santa Claus as the center of interest will delight grown-ups and will also appeal to the childhood faith of the smallest members of the family. (Plates 31, 32).

Buffet settings give opportunity for novel and unusual settings. New ideas are always in the making, so don't hesitate to break away from the usual if in so doing, you develop a plan that is right for *your* table in *your* room. (Plate 24). Keep one important thing in mind: All appointments should be placed on the table so that guests can help themselves conveniently to each dish.

At dinner, grownups would perhaps enjoy a more formal mood. But one thing is important. Throughout all the possibilities of decoration and arrangements, do not overlook that certain something which is expected by those who feel and share the true spirit of the season. Let us call it "emotional appeal." Toward this end, there is no substitute for candlelight in fascination, in elegance, in character, and in subtle beauty. Soft and spreading rays seem to hold benediction, flickering flames cast shadow patterns, mellowing all into a mood of reverence.

candlelight

(plates 33, 34, 35, 36, 37)

Wax from the four corners of the world is fashioned by hand-dipping process or molded (Plate 33) into candles to harmonize in style and hue with any surroundings. (Plate 37). There are, of course, molded candles of the novelty type, but these are better used as ornaments. They lack the handcrafted texture that catches and reflects highlights from surfaces polished by the gleam from candle flame. A note of

29 (Opposite) WHITE CHRISTMAS: *An all-white arrangement with silhouette developed with heavily-whitened manzanita branches; body is added with whitened juniper; accent and contrast of form is given with artificial grapes and foliage painted to match. While the paint was still wet, it was sprayed lightly with plastic "snow" to soften the effect to one of real beauty. The container is milk glass; stands are white, hand-rubbed to a satin finish.*

ARRANGER: MRS. THOMAS STEED PHOTOGRAPHER: OFFIE LITES

warning: keep flame far enough from plant material to avoid fire damage.

Tree ball ornaments of blown glass are versatile material for decoration (Plates 26, 27, 30, 41). At night, the shimmering effect of dancing light on their shiny surfaces is especially attractive, and in daytime, their sparkle can be relied on for charm.

An exquisite red and white decoration is achieved with "sparkle grapes" (real grapes dipped in beaten egg white and then in sugar) on a large red glass plate or platter. Other fruits can be frosted in like manner.

It is novel and beautiful to arrange small fruits and bits of pine on a treelike foundation made from a strip of shiny sheet brass or aluminum, coiled in pyramidal form. To break the severeness, this most modern "tree" looks well resting on a base of pine.

With a large-size birthday-cake candle in a small glass jar, garnish the mealtime tray of a loved one who must spend Christmas Day in bed. A teaspoon of wet plaster of paris secures it to the bottom of the jar. Tiny bits of evergreen and a few bright berries at the base of the candle complete the arrangement.

making mobiles

(plate 30)

For modernists, a Christmas mobile is fascinating. This is made with wire from which a variety of these ornaments are suspended. Constant movement of air in the room keeps the objects swaying gaily to catch constantly new glints of light and to cast a never-ending change of interesting shadows. To be pleasing from all angles, the objects must not dangle haphazardly. Perfect balance is required. To accomplish this, lead shot for weighting is helpful where needed.

And when the blown-glass novelties break, as they do so easily, do not throw them away. When crushed in a paper bag with a rolling pin, they make an exceptionally beautiful "glitter dust" for application to surfaces wet with paint or shellac.

And so, until Twelfth Night, when it is "Down with the bays and ivy all," make merry your Christmas.

30 VERSATILE GLITTER: *Nothing gives more pleasure to the eye than the constant, gentle, playful movement of a Christmas mobile. This charming one is of blown-glass ornaments on a "tree" made from wire in sizes 24, 22, and 18; with lead shot weighting to achieve perfect balance in the objects.*

ARRANGER: MRS. H. G. STATON PHOTOGRAPHER: JEANETTE GROSSMAN

31 (Above) ON THE BREAKFAST TABLE: *An appealing theme—Santa Claus piloting his famous sleigh—this will please adults as well as children. In white, red, and green, with hemlock kept fresh in a container of water concealed with white-edged holly, and with a bag of miniature toys to complete the picture.*

ARRANGER: MRS. F. PALMER HART PHOTOGRAPHER: BOUTRELLE

32 (Right) A JUNIOR CHRISTMAS PARTY: *As symbol of Santa's fabulous slide down the chimney this arrangement will amuse a youngster and inspire him to make a similar one for his own party table. Garnet floribunda roses from the florist, arranged in pleasing size gradation, unify the red of the container with the body of the design. Tall placement of evergreen, thinned out towards the top, emphasizes drama of line and makes a pleasing silhouette.*

ARRANGER: MRS. JOHN M. BURKE PHOTOGRAPHER: JOHN M. BURKE

33 "ONE FOR ADORATION, TWO FOR CELEBRATION": *Spiritual and lovely is this inspired composition against red velvet. Flame gladiolus, gray-green foliage and red bloom of carnations, and small-leaved evergreen branches are kept fresh in water in a concealed pinholder cup. Candles and altar-boy figure are red and white.*

ARRANGER: MRS. JAMES L. FINCH PHOTOGRAPHER: BOUTRELLE

34 ALL IS CALM, ALL IS BRIGHT: *A thick candle burns for hours, symbolizing the light of the world. Nothing is lovelier than its soft rays shining forth from a combination of white or red poinsettias and fresh Christmas green pine branches. The poinsettia, like Helleborus niger the Christmas rose, takes on fresh interest when it is appreciated as legend's miracle flower, transformed from a weed into a gift of love for the little Christ Child. This design is planned to be seen against a wall; an accent of poinsettia in the back will make it attractive from any angle.*

ARRANGER: MRS. H. HENRY STALEY PHOTOGRAPHER: BOUTRELLE

35 THE CHRISTMAS STORY: *Told with symbols of Hope, Faith, and Charity this composition is a pleasing departure from the ordinary. One of the most poignant phrases in the second chapter of Luke says, "there was no room in the inn". Here it is aptly suggested by straw behind the opened Bible. The restraint with which it is used, the simplicity and dignity of the whole arrangement against a bright blue satin background, mark this beautiful design as the work of an artist.*
ARRANGER: MRS. RAYMOND R. STOLTZ PHOTOGRAPHER: BOUTRELLE

36 (Below) CHRISTMAS CANDELABRA: *When there is much to do and little time, one welcomes the easy-to-do. A bough of long-needled pine, holly and berries are attached to a three-branched brass candlestick holding red candles. It is a unique and simple display for almost any place in the home, and symbolic as well, for there are many legends woven around these greens. One that warms the heart, making Christmas and greens inseparable, is their association with fortitude and hardiness; their leaves defy winter's wind and cold.*

ARRANGER: MRS. F. PALMER HART PHOTOGRAPHER: BOUTRELLE

37 (Left) "HAPPY IS THE HOME IN WHICH BAYBERRIES BURN": *Against an antique mold burnished with gold and holding three bayberry candles, the arranger applies her art in rich, soft tones to a crescent design of Scotch broom, branches heavily-jewelled with gray bayberries, juniper, acorns and pine cones tinted gray-green and touched with gold.*
ARRANGER: MRS. E. R. VAN LIEW PHOTOGRAPHER: JOHN MAXON

38 (Below) SERENITY: *Madonna and Child rest on a wooden pedestal painted to match gray bases and waxed to a rich, mellow patina. Container is made from plumbers' lead molded into a shape with fluted edge. Atlas cedar, Royal Silver Oregon holly, traditional white chrysanthemums, and snowberries are the plant materials. The chrysanthemum is most appropriate in Christmas decoration for legend gives it beautiful significance—the little white flower was born on the first Christmas, its beauty shining to guide the wise men to the baby Jesus.*
ARRANGER: MRS. E. R. VAN LIEW PHOTOGRAPHER: CHARLES F. CYPHERS

39 A BEAUTIFUL GIFT TO THE CHILD WHOSE BIRTH WE CELEBRATE: *The heart of the Nativity is manifested warmly in this unusual color plan. Heather in lavender and purple tones, roses and carnations in pink, and spruce in blue-gray-green are arranged to partially encircle a lovely figure of Madonna and Child in tones of mauve. Staged against wine-red velvet background, this Christmas sentiment is enhanced in warmth and richness.*

ARRANGER: MRS. JAMES L. FINCH PHOTOGRAPHER: BOUTRELLE

40 "HARK! THE HERALD ANGELS SING": *Inspired by the simple and joyous manner in which Christ's birth and missions are revealed in the beautiful hymn by Charles Wesley, the arranger used the circular pattern, symbol of eternal life, as background for a cherished Madonna in a pose of adoration. To make the wreath,* *see page 41.*

ARRANGER: MRS. CLIFFORD E. CYPHERS PHOTOGRAPHER: CHARLES F. CYPHERS

41 GAYNESS IN A BASEMENT "WHOOPEE" ROOM: *A splash of brilliance against soft gray-green concrete walls expresses a joyous mood. The sculptured "minister of grace" replica strums a mandolin in accompaniment with musical gongs of shiny brass echoed in gold tree balls against gray-green plant material.*

ARRANGER: MRS. CLIFFORD E. CYPHERS PHOTOGRAPHER: CHARLES F. CYPHERS

42 ONE FOR THE BIRDS: *Plastic "snow" gently sprayed softens this arrangement. To enhance the Christmas scene, a red ceramic cardinal perched among branches of dark green yew and rhododendron leaves, garnet-red dried cones of berried sumac, and fascinating nest-like shapes of dried Queen Anne's lace bring inside a bit of the great outdoors.*

ARRANGER: MRS. LOUIS H. AMER PHOTOGRAPHER: CARPENTER'S STUDIO

43 (Left) APPEALING THEME: *Sprayed with "snow", a branch of white pine and a grouping of cones complement a lovely hand-carved figure of a girl and bird to enrich Yuletide sentiment in the home.*

ARRANGER: MRS. JAMES L. FINCH PHOTOGRAPHER: BOUTRELLE

44 (Below) ACCENT ON THE OUT-OF-DOORS: *This subdued color scheme tells an appropriate story. Inspired by a wood's scene, the arranger used a graceful manzanita branch to symbolize a "winter tree"; Scotch pine, and evergreen. Pine cones grouped casually and wired in place on twigs contribute interest, as does the lovely deer, so much a part of Christmas tradition.*

ARRANGER: MRS. LOUIS H. AMER PHOTOGRAPHER: CARPENTER'S STUDIO

45 BEAUTY IN GREEN AND BROWN: *Suited to many locations in the home, a pair of beautifully hand-carved deer complete an exquisite composition with berried juniper, manzanita, and dried Hawaiian "roses". Distinction is apparent in hue and texture relationship. Of special note is the light tan on the inside petals of the roses, repeated in the hue of the plaque's flat surface, in light touches on the manzanita branch, and in the wooden figures with brown of the outer petals echoed on the branch, and on the edges of the plaque.*

ARRANGER: MRS. JOHN W. KNIGHT, JR. PHOTOGRAPHER: DWITE A. WALKER

46 ST. FRANCIS OF ASSISI: *The Christmas crèche is a favored Noël decoration and in many homes is given a place of honor. It is appropriate to pay esteem to the man responsible for the very first such scene, the patron saint of woodland creatures. Using live figures to depict the Nativity, St. Francis taught the Christmas story to village folk. Here in brown, gray, and gray-green, a woodland setting pays tribute to him. A root of tree has been fashioned into a candle holder at the base of which is grouped "flowers" made of fungus petals sewn together into rosettes. The ceramic figure is a sculptor's version of the saint.*

ARRANGER: MRS. CLIFFORD E. CYPHERS PHOTOGRAPHER: CHARLES F. CYPHERS

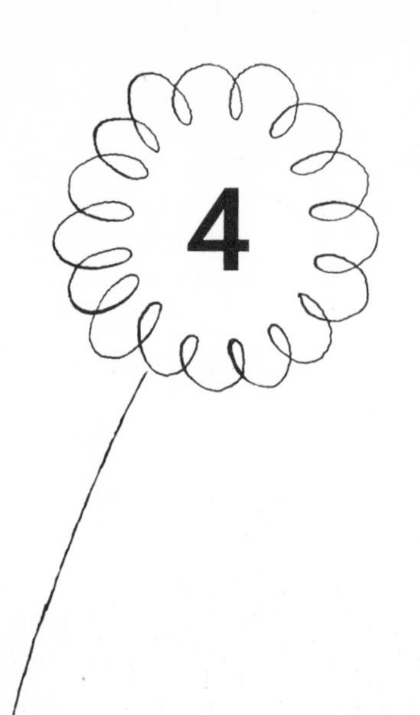

Easter

FLOWERS ARE THE ESSENTIAL ELEMENT

As winter points toward spring, everyone succumbs to the spell of the coming Eastertide. Easter—the very word gladdens our hearts and spirits. Though its name is derived from paganism, Christians the world over observe the day in holy reverence of Christ's ascent to an Eternal Life. In the early days of Christianity, there were those who were willing to accept the new faith but reluctant to disclaim their spring goddess, Eastre. She, they believed, brought the warmth of sunshine into the world when doves hatched her from a large egg descended from heaven. Christ arose from the tomb on the Sabbath, although the actual date is not accounted for. So it is not surprising that Christian priests appeased the people by retaining the Saxon festival in Eastre's honor, but used it in holy commemoration of the Resurrection and called the day on which it was held, Easter.

Falling as it does on the first Sunday following the first paschal full moon after March 21, observance of the Easter festival varies over a

48 (Below) PEACE ON EARTH: *On a white styrofoam (plastic) base, yew and ivy leaves contrast their dark green hue with white of the trumpet-like lilies, painted hawthorn branches, and a pair of doves to interpret the meaning of Easter.*

ARRANGER: MRS. GERSON T. HIRSCH PHOTOGRAPHER: BOUTRELLE

47 (Above) SIMPLE GRANDEUR ON EASTER: *A white alabaster urn holds lilies and Funkia foliage. The lily is recorded as a sacred flower as far as its history can be traced. To the ancient Greeks it was a symbol of their goddess, Hera; to the Romans, it was the flower of their goddess, Juno. When Christianity replaced paganism, missionaries found it advantageous to retain pagan customs, fitting them into the new religious rites—hence the Easter lily was designated to the Virgin, and became a symbol of chasteness and benevolence.*

ARRANGER: MRS. F. PALMER HART PHOTOGRAPHER: BOUTRELLE

49 TO REFLECT AN EASTER MOOD: *An asymmetrical arrangement of foliage and chalice-like bloom of calla lilies in a handmade pewter plate expresses a simple inspiration. A small inverted dish raises it, adding to an air of importance.*
ARRANGER: MRS. GEORGE J. HIRSCH PHOTOGRAPHER: SEAF

period of thirty-five days. But it is significant that it takes place at the year's morn, when an awakening earth proclaims the promise of flowers soon to come. Flowers, so radiantly pure, belong to Easter, and just as surely flowers should be the essential element in your decorations for symbolic celebration.

flowers on Easter
(plates 51, 52, 53)

The always-available carnation is an excellent choice for Easter decoration. It looks well in almost any container and in any location in the home. Of course, Easter lilies are the symbolical flowers of the day. Whether you use a dozen or only three, they suggest the gladness and triumph of Eastertide. White bloom is always good at this time. Remember that this day, closing the solemn season of Lent, is one of great rejoicing.

Easter symbolism in accessories

Like all holidays, Easter has a share of symbolic motifs that play a part in decoration. Among the most popular is the egg, in recognition of the one from which the goddess Eastre was born, and the bunny, which is the symbol of fertility. But from the tapestry of fact and fantasy woven through the centuries by people of many nations, it is the baby chicks and ducks, the "little things" (Plates 48, 53) that awaken the most universal response. And children love them, appropriately so, for these appealing creatures are sweet and gentle as they themselves.

On Easter when flowers are available in profusion of form and hue, it is thoughtlessness, not lack of reverence, that leads to decorative ostentation. Keep in mind a simple and serene beauty that spiritual expression can impart; restraint and dignity are in character on Easter.

condition plant material

Flowers from a reliable florist are well conditioned to preserve their fresh, crisp quality and can be arranged without further attention. Cut from the garden, however, material must be "hardened" to insure the longest possible life.

First, a word or two about picking. Commercial growers have scorned old superstitions regarding the time of day for picking, but they advise cutting flowers in bud stage for three reasons. The bloom lasts longer; the flower tissues are not broken; the purity of hue is retained.

After severing the stems from the mother plant, cut them again under water and on a slant. Then soak the stems in deep, cool water for an hour or two before arranging. Stems that exude a sticky or milky substance require the special treatment suggested on page 37 for conditioning poinsettias. Plants with pithy or tough stems, like hydrangeas, or with pithy foliage, like dahlias, should be treated in the same manner, or plunged to a depth of about two inches into scalding water for one minute and then into cool water for the soaking period. When in doubt about a flower's lasting qualities, do not hesitate to use the hot-water treatment. Heat hurries the rise of water and acts as a stimulant.

Foliage benefits greatly by complete immersion in cool water during the soaking period. This is a *must* for conditioning ferns.

Semiwoody stems, like the peony and chrysanthemum, require three or four inches of the stem end to be crushed. The rose is an exception. Its water absorber is but a thin membrane between the heart and outer covering on the stem, and to expose as much as possible is advantageous. To do so, cut off the thorns, or make slits at intervals on that part of the stem that will be under water in the completed design.

Prevent quick wilting of bloom or foliage on woody branches by scraping off several inches of bark on the end of the branch, and/or cutting a slit upward for an inch or two before soaking.

forced material is useful

Now is the logical time to use cut branches from trees and shrubs forced into bloom or leafage within the home. Almost any branch can be hastened into growth if sprays are cut at least eighteen inches long. The longer the branch, the more sap can rise into the buds, and the easier it is to force. Peel the bark for two to three inches from the ends of the branches, and place them in deep water. An occasional spraying or complete immersion in tepid water hastens the forcing process.

Following is a list of varieties that force well, with approximate time required in a temperature of 65 to 70 degrees.

Shrub or Tree	Approximate Time
Andromeda	12 days
Azalea	16 days
Barberry	23 days
Bayberry	26 days
Cercis (redbud)	26 days
Cornus (dogwood)	23 days
Corylus (hazelnut)	16 days
Cydonia (flowering quince)	23 days
Fruiting apple	29 days
Fruiting cherry, pear, plum	22 days
Flowering almond	20 days
Flowering cherry, crab apple, peach	23 days
Forsythia	18 days
Horse chestnut	14 days
Huckleberry	23 days
Magnolia soulangeana (long sprays required)	20 days
Magnolia stellata	20 days
Maple, red	14 days
Paulownia (empress tree)	26 days
Poplar	7 days
Pussy willow	12 days
Shadbush	15 days
Spiraea (bridal wreath)	23 days
Syringa (lilac)	30 days
Viburnum (common snowball)	6 weeks

50 EXPRESSION OF JOY: *Imaginative yet practical decoration is reflected in this unusual and inspired design composed within the dignity of a pyramidal boundary on a chartreuse disc. Gray-green succulent echeveria foliage rosettes catch the eye as center of interest. The eye moves along an ascending line through the flowers to shoots of bamboo arranged in organ-pipe formation.*

ARRANGER: MRS. GEORGE GOLDSON PHOTOGRAPHER: LUCI BLATT

51 RICH WITH THE SEASON'S HUES: *Refined foliage of gardenia enhances snapdragons and tulips in values of pink, and Dutch iris in white. Ingenuity displayed in the contrived "skyscraper" container is noteworthy—one of two clear glass cake stands is inverted on the other and supports a crystal vase on its upside-down base.*

ARRANGER: MRS. RHYNOLD G. SCHULKE PHOTOGRAPHER: HARRY W. SCHULKE

52 IN EASTER COLORS OF YELLOW AND VIOLET: *"Return Engagement" titles this entertaining composition designed as a tribute to Spring. The sunshine hue in tulips, daffodils, and snapdragons is emphasized by a bunch of spring violets at the center of interest. A goldfinch with her mate beside their nest, nestled snugly in fascinatingly-textured bark, strengthens the story-telling theme. Pussy willow, a harbinger of the spring season, adds height and aesthetic satisfaction.*
ARRANGER: MRS. EDWARD A. WHITE PHOTOGRAPHER: BOUTRELLE

53 "A TISKET, A TASKET, A BROWN AND YELLOW BASKET": *Early yellow-green flowers of a maple tree, yellow and creamy white daffodils, white andromeda in single and double varieties, and green euonymus branches are combined in a natural reed basket on a tray woven of the same material but stained brown. The butterfly repeats the yellow-green and brown. Plant material at the base is kept fresh in concealed tubes of water.*
ARRANGER: MRS. LOUIS H. AMER PHOTOGRAPHER: CARPENTER'S STUDIO

54 "HOPE REBORN! IT'S EASTER DAY!": *Shiny bronze-tipped Mahonia foliage, new bronzy growth of maple, and giant yellow crocus with its spiked leaves, are arranged in a dark red-brown basket on a natural fiber mat base. Eggs dyed yellow and broken, the inside colored in a deeper tone, are intriguing. These are wired on sticks and used to bring emphasis at the focus of attention.*

ARRANGER: MRS. LOUIS H. AMER PHOTOGRAPHER: CARPENTER'S STUDIO

55 (Left) EASTER NOVELTY: *With a background painted to simulate a bit of sky, a pink cart carrying pink flowers and a "blue bird of happiness" perched inquiringly on its side, this composition creates a happy, carefree mood. Plant materials are pink snapdragons and peonies, peony foliage, and leucothoe.*

ARRANGER: MRS. DAVID KIRSCHENBAUM PHOTOGRAPHER: BOUTRELLE

56 (Right) FOR THE YOUNG AT HEART: *On a brass tray, a chocolate bunny and eggs dyed brown, tan, and green, blend with hues of other materials in this Easter greeting. Plant materials: French pussy willows, Mahonia, Galax, and succulents.*

ARRANGER: MRS. LOUIS H. AMER PHOTOGRAPHER: CARPENTER'S STUDIO

Celebrations Around the Calendar

USE EACH SEASON'S
OFFERINGS FOR HOLIDAY ARRANGEMENTS

Season by season, the year circles around, measured by celebrated days to honor great men or great events, historical or legendary. From the beloved and hallowed days in the Christian calendar, we move to other holidays generally observed.

It is logical to return to the year's first celebration—the beginning of a brand-new year full of promise for all. In America, January 1 is a time for general entertaining and visiting. Open house and social calls on friends and neighbors are in order, with the exchange of good wishes and merrymaking that has been the custom for observing the festal New Year since the dawn of civilization.

warmth and gaiety for New Year's Day
(plates 57, 58)

Because January 1 begins the coldest and, to some, the dreariest month of the year (though a dried plum to one who says so!) is all

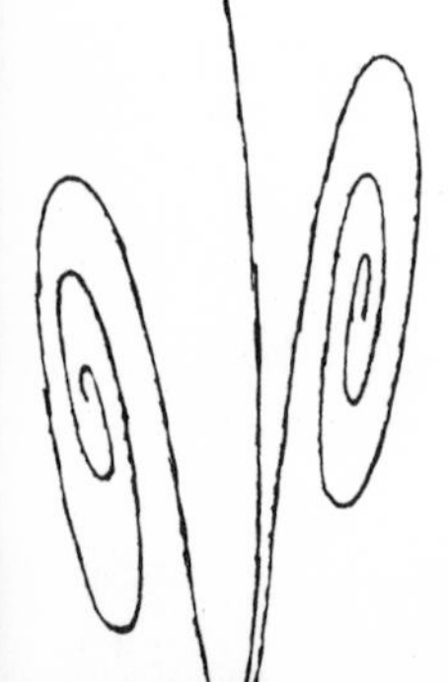

57 (Right) RADIANT REFLECTIONS: *January 1 is a day for spiritual examination. To express this personal feeling the arranger has combined vitex, bougainvillea, billbergia nutans, and aloe variegata in a copper container, and has placed the arrangement on a mirror base to reflect the design's radiating pattern.*

ARRANGER: MRS. EDGAR LITTMANN PHOTOGRAPHER: ELLIS LITTMANN

58 FLOWERS FOR THE LADIES ON NEW YEAR'S DAY: *Twigs of silver beech to simulate a tree are securely fastened with floral clay to a mirrored base. Green satin ribbon ties together tiny white dried flowers (a weed) in corsage fashion. They are wired to the branches to be given later, one to each guest. More ribbon and flowers with silvered juniper add weight, body, and drama to this unique decoration on the tea table.*

ARRANGER: MRS. LOUIS H. AMER
PHOTOGRAPHER: EDWARD MAHER

the more reason for warm and glowing decoration in the home. By now the shimmer of Christmas decoration may be tarnishing and will no longer meet your needs on this gala occasion. Decoration should be as fresh, as bright, and as crisp as New Year resolutions, for like those resolutions, they won't be kept for long!

In a spirit of gaiety, let your decorations gleam, glitter, and shine even brighter than on Christmas, for New Year's Day is a final fling to the exhilarant mood. All too soon the world slips back into a quieter frame of mind, when more subdued decorations are easier to live with day by day.

On the eve of a coming year's first day, your decoration can be joyous and gay. This is the month dedicated to Janus, Roman god of doors and gates. With two heads, Janus saw into the past and future at one time, and so through the centuries, man has looked upon the eve of the new year with happy and cheerful expectations. Tomorrow, life's realities may sober all; tonight, the world is carefree. Decorations that display this carousel touch through the use of gilt paint, sparkle dust, and gay paper streamers will not be wearying, for the New Year celebration lasts but a short, short time.

Bells, emblems of hospitality, by tradition "ring out the old, ring in the new." In New Year arrangements, the bell tolls out the joys of a year just past, of all years past, of all the years to come.

patriotism a theme for February

February, the shortest month, gave America two illustrious statesmen. A patriotic theme should be expressed in your decoration paying tribute to George Washington and to Abraham Lincoln. The sharp contrasts in red, white and blue require careful handling to bring their unrelated attributes into harmony within the design. It has been said that intense spectrum hues should not be combined without harmonizing through a stepping-down sequence in tonal value. But positive statements are often false. In trying to be explicit, one is not always accurate. In this color problem, white will serve as a unifier, and success in your design will be a matter of proportion rather than of variation in the intensity of the spectrum red and blue.

In design, an unequal division of hues observes the principle of dominance referred to in Chapter 1. A graded measure in areas of hue, with one for character (dominance), one for interest (contrast), and one for its relative size (rhythm), assures the pleasure and satisfaction that is natural in the growing plant (Plate 60).

dignified patriotism for Memorial Day
(plate 60)

Memorial Day, originally called Decoration Day, is one of the reverent days in the year, and unlike most patriotic observances, restraint and dignified simplicity, rather than gaiety, take precedence. After the Civil War, the Southern States honored the battle dead with flowers scattered in solemn ceremony on their graves. The North was soon to follow suit, and May 30 was declared Decoration Day in memory of those gallant men who sacrificed their lives. Confederate Memorial Day is honored in Virginia on May 30; Alabama, Florida, Georgia and

59 TRIBUTE TO ABRAHAM LINCOLN: *Atmospheric tones of lavender and purple in the gladiolus, dahlias, and dracaena leaves enhance a fine bronze statue of Abraham Lincoln and emphasize his pose of meditation, the inspired theme of this lovely expressive composition. Elevated as it is on velvet steps, an appropriate and significant decoration is achieved to honor a great American on his birthday.*

ARRANGER: MRS. DAVID KIRSCHENBAUM PHOTOGRAPHER: WILLIAM ALLEN

60 STAR PATTERN FOR PATRIOTS: *This table arrangement on Memorial Day strikes a patriotic note in red, white, and blue. Flowers are blue delphinium, red peonies, and white calla lilies. It was designed for use on a medium light blue cloth, and with red napkins. Individual place settings included Spode's "Blue Tower" china, crystal, and silver.*

ARRANGER: MISS RAE PENNINGTON PHOTOGRAPHER: HAMMOND PORTRAIT STUDIO

Mississippi on April 26; Kentucky and North Carolina on May 10; Louisiana and Tennessee on June 3. But it makes little difference which day you observe, remembering is the same for all.

June 14 is Flag Day

Flag Day is observed on the anniversary of the adoption of the Stars and Stripes by Congress on June 14, 1777. When the American flag is used in decoration, standards set by the National Flag Conference should be adopted.

Arrange your flowers in the casual manner of the Colonial period in American history, in memory of Betsy Ross who made the first flag of our country.

symbolic Fourth of July colors

The drama of a symbolic red, white, and blue scheme is appropriate for decoration on July 4, our nation's birthday. Its force of contrast has an exhilarating effect on our emotions. The combination can be as exciting as the event it commemorates.

Coming as it does in the hot month, the month of bright sunlight and high temperature, Independence Day affords the opportunity for outdoor entertainment of friends or just lazy enjoyment of the family. Meet the challenge to your ingenuity and skill by planning your decoration for the sun and breeze or for the moon and stars. Harden your flowers to withstand the wilting rays of the sun. Plan your design in a horizontal plane to withstand the wind in case Zephyrus blows his breath with force. At night, an all-white arrangement will be a a special source of pleasure. When lights are dim and the family relaxes outdoors in the cool and calm of a nighttime world, the moonlight will enhance the clean, fresh brightness of white bloom.

the value of white

Never underestimate the power of white flowers. White is a "color" that may be expressive of various moods. Used alone, it is serene and

61 BRED OF JOY AND GRATITUDE: *For various reasons people from many lands come to America. Whatever the lure that brings them, America extends welcome. And at her feet these strangers lay native customs and traditions—the result is a country rich in festal heritage. This composition, symbolic of welcome, opportunity, and abundance within our boundaries, is fitting tribute on Independence Day, the day commemorating the nation's birth.*
ARRANGER: MRS. GEORGE J. HIRSCH
PHOTOGRAPHER: BOUTRELLE

restful. Combined with bright hue, the area it occupies increases in apparent size, its whiteness emphasized. Combined with golden yellows, white is warmed. It is cooled with greens and blues.

mass arrangements for Columbus Day
(plate 62)

By October 12, most flowers in the garden are bedraggled. However, marigolds, zinnias, and chrysanthemums are available to provide ample floral material. Mass arrangements of these flowers give colorful and appropriate autumn decoration.

In your design, the group of flowers as a whole is more important than any single bloom in it, but this does not indicate haphazard placement. The loveliest arrangements are made up of many well-balanced units combined in beautiful effects. There is a center of interest to aid in achieving unity, and some line structure is evident. Flowers and foliage are combined chiefly for color and textural interest, and overcrowding is avoided in the best examples.

Army Day in April and Navy Day in October

Army Day, April 6, since 1927 has commemorated the day that the United States joined the Allies in World War I. And Navy Day too,

62 (Opposite) COLUMBUS DAY DESIGN: *Appropriate tribute to the man who reached our shores in 1492, a coconut spathe "vessel" is mounted on a block to establish linear flow. I's fibrous surface with wood filler was stained brown, harmonizing with the small plates and standards of goblets holding pink cups. The pink is repeated in the flowers; the green of the linen is in the tropical foliage. Bamboo-trimmed yellow plates and a handmade red candle with pink overlay add distinction.*

ARRANGER: MRS. SAMUEL LASKER PHOTOGRAPHER: BOUTRELLE

63 (Above) EXCITING AS A PARADE: *Complementary hues, bright red of gladiolus and anthuriums, and green of philodendron and gladiolus foliage, present forceful contrast to portray an exhilarant mood. The spiked leaves of gladiolus are tied in knots to swing the eye outward thereby giving a feeling of motion. The antique pistol strong enough in shape, in hue, and in substance to arrest attention and keep the eye within the picture is placed across a wedge-shaped piece of pink granite, symbol of our country's strength.*

ARRANGER: MRS. A. F. STUEBING PHOTOGRAPHER: BUROIN

commemorates a comparatively young celebration. Since 1922, public-spirited citizens have watched "maneuvers of ships and naval aircraft, and reviews of naval militia" on October 27, the birthday of Theodore Roosevelt who realized the importance of the navy as the "First line of Defense."

Armistice Day

The serious, gentle mood is also appropriate for Armistice Day, November 11, dedicated to cessation of hostilities in World War I. Decorations are simple and solemn in mood, and flowers and accessories, combined perhaps with patriotic symbols and colors, pay tribute to the hope for eternal peace among all nations of the earth.

Mother's Day in May and Father's Day in June

(plates 64, 65, 66, 67, 68, 69, 70)

The massed design is well chosen, also, for decoration on these special days set apart for remembering our parents (Plate 64). The second Sunday in May dignifies motherhood; the third in June, fatherhood. The occasions are gay ones tempered only by solemn reminiscence.

The fullest appreciation of what motherhood stands for comes in religion. Keep in mind its simple dignity, and you will avoid doing the right thing in the wrong way when arranging flowers to the memory of your mother (Plate 65). Maintain the beauty of a dignified conception in arrangement, and yet reflect the emotional quality of the day. Your arrangements can be full in design, but not crowded or complex. Let them be radiant and rich in hue, but not garish or intense.

As established, carnations, pink or white depending on whether one's mother is living or deceased, are the accepted traditional flowers on Mother's Day. Nevertheless, it is just as fitting to honor her with an arrangement of her favorite bloom and hue as in Plate 65.

64 (Opposite) TO MOTHER ON HER SPECIAL DAY: *This tribute to a beloved mother has a richness and splendor as grand as the age which marked her happiest days. Red carnations and gladiolus, white stock, and white-spotted and silvery begonia foliage are arranged with dignity in a formal alabaster urn. Orchid tubes of water keep flowers and leaves fresh at the base of the arrangement. Picture and bible are appropriate contributions to the character of the whole.*

ARRANGER: MRS. THOMAS STEED PHOTOGRAPHER: OFFIE LITES

65 "FAIR AS A ROSE WAS SHE": *As a variation of the traditional carnation tribute on Mother's Day, her favorite blooms, Talisman roses, are enhanced by their own lush, bronzy foliage and arranged in crystal to express sweet and treasured memories.*

ARRANGER: MRS. GEORGE J. HIRSCH PHOTOGRAPHER: MICHAEL G. SPOTO

One dexterous arranger whom I know departed from the ordinary in honoring her mother, active in ornithology. She used blue birds (for happiness, you know) made of china as the dominant feature of a composition, with flowers playing supporting cast. Such schemes are fun to plan and stimulating on father's day too. (Plate 69).

Roses are designated as flowers for Father's Day (Plate 68). Significantly, very red roses are favored because the name "Adam" means red, emblem of human life.

flowers combined with other material

In spite of some misguided opinion, flowers playing second fiddle, as it were, can result in work both beautiful and logical. The important thing is that when flowers are combined with other substances—fruit, dried plant material, or inanimate objects—one or the other should predominate. Remember the principle of dominance for complete design satisfaction (Plates 70, 88).

Remember, too, that your arrangement should have a starting point to attract the eye in its easy rhythmic path through a design. This is the center of interest and is supplied by a contrast in shape, size, hue, or texture, as in the little china birds in the composition described above. A center of interest is evident in all illustrations in this book.

flowers and fruit for Labor Day
(plates 71, 72)

The first Monday in September is a legal rest day for those who labor. This means Labor Day is for you! Decorate your home, inspired by the sky as limit! Flowers are plentiful, and almost any combination will make a good arrangement providing it is designed as an artist paints his canvas, that is, with consideration for harmony and unity in the completed composition. This, too, is a reminder that the eye sees clearly only one thing at a time; that a design gains in effectiveness if it "fits" not only in character or theme, but in size as well. An arrangement too large for its space appears crowded and cramped. Too small, it is dwarfed sometimes to insignificance. Proportion need not be difficult if you train yourself to truly see the natural proportion in plant life. This will help you to develop an innate sense of good proportion.

66 (Abovc) EFFECTIVE SIMPLICITY: *Here, in a nostalgic mood, are roses arranged with feathery evergreen branches in a brass teakettle on a matching brass tray base. Crumpled chicken wire (one-inch mesh is best) in the receptacle holds the material in place. This represents an arrangement "so easy to make", says Mrs. Burke, "that even a child could do it".*

ARRANGER: MRS. JOHN M. BURKE PHOTOGRAPHER: JOHN M. BURKE

67 (Right) FOR A MODERN MOTHER: *Bridal wreath fastened in loops, white and creamy-white tulips and variegated pointed ovals of hosta leaves are vertically arranged in a horizontally-shaped black bowl to contrast in shape and tonal value, distinguishing features of contemporary art.*

ARRANGER: MRS. LOUIS H. AMER PHOTOGRAPHER: CARPENTER'S STUDIO

68 RED ROSES FOR FATHER: *In an arrangement of strength and vitality, rich glowing red New Yorker roses contrast with bright green Scotch broom. Willowy eucalyptus supplies texture interest. The container is an antique Oriental bronze incense burner.*

ARRANGER: MRS. JOHN W. KNIGHT, JR. PHOTOGRAPHER: DWITE A. WALKER

69 TRIBUTE TO DAD: *The favored custom of "red carnations on Fathers' Day" has carried over into this clever composition emphasizing dad's favorite pastime. Branches of pineapple-guava shrub are used with grayish underside of leaves prominent to echo the gray of the tackle box container. Garden mullein adds another gray. Flowers are red carnations. Red and white lures accentuate the idea.*
ARRANGER: MRS. THOMAS STEED PHOTOGRAPHER: OFFIE LITES

70 INSPIRED BY DAD'S FAVORITE PRINT: *This attractive composition especially for dad is suited to a favored spot in his den, his study or, for that matter, in the family living room. To compliment the Audubon print, swamp cattail and iris with their leaves and hosta foliage are combined in a natural growth pattern.*
ARRANGER: MRS. JAMES L. FINCH PHOTOGRAPHER: BOUTRELLE

71 (Above) A LABOR DAY BASKET: *Though not for long, flowers still abound in the garden on Labor Day, so it is logical to enjoy an open and airy mass arrangement like this one of wheat, daisies, small yellow sunflowers, green berries, and rhododendron foliage combined and staged on a woven basket tray. Water receptacle is a tuna-fish tin painted to render it inconspicuous. When the use of many flowers is appropriate, if you value the familiar forms, hues, and textures you can achieve beauty without cash for rare containers or exotic plant material.*

ARRANGER: MRS. LOUIS H. AMER PHOTOGRAPHER: CARPENTER'S STUDIO

Dahlias and gladiolus are key blooms around Labor Day, and annual flowers—asters, marigolds, zinnias, snapdragons, celosia—are still available to offer a wide range of color and shape. Much of this season's bloom is bold in form, rich in hue, and rugged in texture. Solid massed effects can be saved from a heavy look by introducing glossy leaves or fruits.

Fruits are now beginning to be harvested. Beautiful patterns are achieved when their interesting shapes and surface textures are combined with flowers. Such combinations are especially attractive on the dining terrace or for barbecue buffet. Labor Day week end in many states offers almost the last opportunity for outdoor meals.

72 SETTING FOR A BARBECUE BUFFET: *Amusing accessories are appropriate for a gala barbecue buffet on the terrace. Flowers are well hardened and arranged in containers which hold ample water to last remarkably well in outdoor heat. The height of the arrangement requires a location protected from wind. In a bowl concealed on a copper plaque, sorghum red sunflowers, yellow squashes and tomatoes, and tin roosters painted mat black, tie in beautifully with wrought-iron terrace furniture.*

ARRANGER: MRS. RHYNOLD G. SHULKE PHOTOGRAPHER: HARRY W. SHULKE

Fun-Scored and Intimate Days

COMBINE HUMOR AND NOVELTY IN INTIMATE DECORATIONS

"Holiday" according to the dictionary, means, as a noun, "a consecrated, a religious day, a day of exemption from labor" and as an adjective, "pertaining to a festival, gay." Some of the latter, with fun and intimacy as key factors, will be interpreted here in relation to decoration in the home.

Halloween and All Saints' Day

(plates 73, 74, 75, 76, 77)

Halloween—"All hallow Eve"—the night before the Feast of All Saints' Day, is a favored one for entertaining. In ancient times, huge bonfires were lighted to frighten away evil ghosts and witches. Today, in the spirit of fun, people still attempt escape from the mischievous

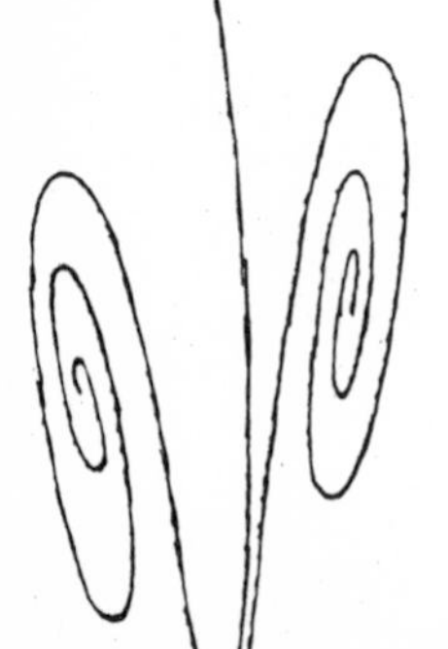

pranks of unwelcome demons. When the harvest moon hung high and large, pagan Romans held a festival in honor of happy Pomona, goddess of fruits. Apples were her favorite and so have always been associated with Halloween. Her appreciation is responsible for today's fun-filled sport of bobbing for them. Yes, this is a time for fun! Decorations are planned to invite it. Anything that takes away from the humorous intrigue of mystery and merriment is to be deplored.

dried forms for Halloween

(plate 75)

By October 31, color in the garden for the most part has given way to form—skeletal and geometric structural substances of flower and leaf. The beautiful symmetry in design of seed pods often rivals that of the fresh flower and is constantly a lure. Each season reveals a material distinctly different from that of other seasons, a material that sets a mood. And now a certain mysterious elegance of dried forms fits the spirit of the goblins' hour.

To increase your supply, it is farsighted to gather flowers and leaves throughout the growing season, to dry them and store them for use

73 WELCOME GHOSTS AND GOBLINS: *For fun-filled hearts that are light and free, this composition makes one believe in black magic! Green ti leaves are swirled to simulate the curl in a cat's tail. Croton foliage in mixed yellow and green is transition between them and red anthurium used to symbolize fire flame. Black cats, ghost-like Spanish moss, and spider lend mystery and weirdness. To force leaves to take on desired curves, lay a straight wire along the center rib and fasten in place with corsage floral tape that matches in hue. It is a simple matter now to curl the inconspicuously-wired leaves into desired pattern.*

ARRANGER: MRS. FRANCES DIGI PHOTOGRAPHER: BOUTRELLE

in your arrangements of late fall. There are few garden blooms that cannot be dried to retain their hue although it may be muted. Instructions for drying the more difficult with borax are found in books on dried arrangements, available in libraries or bookstores. For easy to dry materials, avoid the fully blown flowers, for ripening of the seed cannot be stopped in the too-old bloom. Hang the cut flowers in loose bundles, heads down, in a hot, dry, but airy place to hasten drying, which helps to retain some natural color. Slow drying results in subtle gray, beige, or brown tones. Stems will dry in curves if you place them over a large rounded form or mold them with your fingers from time to time during the drying period.

74 A CHANGE FROM ORANGE AND BLACK WITH BATS: A *Halloween merrymaking—when young people masked and costumed visit from one house to another—is suggested in this four-foot design for an important spot near the entrance. Its coloring against a violet-gray wall suggests moonlight, emphasized with blue floodlight. Materials: Branch of cedar with blueberries; partly charred silver-gray cedar root; purple-bronze life mask of an Indian witch.*
ARRANGER: GRACE COYLE PHOTOGRAPHER: BOUTRELLE

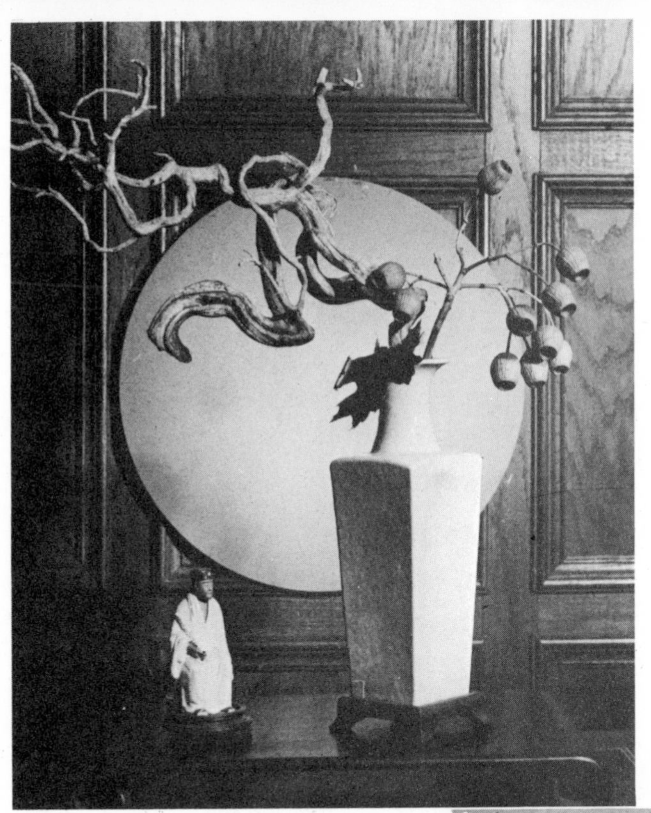

75 (Left) HARVEST MOON: *Thoughts on Halloween are a mixture of Druid superstitions, classic mythology, and Christian belief. The arranger combines them in an original interpretation appropriate to hall or living room. Materials, all dried except the colorful autumn oak leaves, include brown eucalyptus pods; weathered manzanita branch; Chinese celadon vase; mandarin; silver disk.*

ARRANGER: MRS. EDGAR LITTMANN PHOTOGRAPHER: WALTER SKRAINKA

76 (Below) FOR ALL SAINTS' DAY: *Here one sees a composition based on religious theme in its suggestion of a church shrine with candles. In Louisiana the day following Allhallows Eve is observed by decorating graves, a habit developed in all probability from custom brought to the state by Acadians settled there.*

ARRANGER: MRS. ALBERT P. MICCICHE PHOTOGRAPHER: ELEMORE MORGAN

77 "ST. FRANCIS AND THE BIRDS": *A distinctive and original mark in this composition is the interesting container contrived by using two in one—an orange-colored, handmade pottery bowl within one of tortoise shell. Strelitzia, familiarly known as Bird of Paradise, in orange and violet-blue tones, is combined with its own foliage in pattern radiating from behind the ceramic figure of the saint.*
ARRANGER: MRS. EDGAR LITTMANN PHOTOGRAPHER: CHARLES TREFTS

78 A VALENTINE TO SMILE A WELCOME: *Gay flowers and ferns grouped in design against a lace-edged milk-glass plate create a festive look. The plate stands on a wire rack. This simple and appealing plan would be charming on almost any occasional table, or on a mantel.*

ARRANGER: MRS. LOUIS H. AMER PHOTOGRAPHER: CARPENTER'S STUDIO

79 HE LOVES ME, HE LOVES ME NOT: *Informality is in the air with a Valentine token such as shown here. A few sprigs of yew and a cluster of amiable daisies grouped around a sweet and lovely small bisque cupid are all you need to make a pleasing arrangement.*

ARRANGER: SENTA KOPF PHOTOGRAPHER: BOUTRELLE

be sentimental on Valentine's Day
(plates 78, 79, 80)

A challenge to your ingenuity comes during the winter months. By giving your imagination full sway, you can meet February with artistic expressions of varied concept. In stars and stripes, hearts and cupids, flags and eagles, or lace and frills, you will find inspiration for your arrangements. And there are candles in the offing, too.

We have already discussed patriotic arrangements to commemorate the birthdays of America's favorite statesmen born in February. But February gives us Valentine's Day as well, when the "sterner stuff" is replaced with emphasis on sentiment, established by custom and legend to pay tribute to lovers, young and old. All the world loves lovers, and February 14 is their day. Why, I wonder, do so

80 LOVERS' MELODY: *Staid and ancient tradition is symbolized with lovely Venetian figures, red flecked with gold picked up in golden acacia. Narcissus is white with yellow cups. An ethereal quality is gained by spreading downy winged milkweed seeds around the figures. Cupid's red sash draws the eye to the bow which repeats the diagonal rhythm of the top of the forsythia branch.*
ARRANGER: MRS. SAMUEL LASKER
PHOTOGRAPHER: BOUTRELLE

many conceal their feeling for the sentimental? How cold and empty are lives without it! Inspired by Dan Cupid's contribution of sweetness, let hearts and flowers and frills and romance bloom boldly and gaily on this day.

candles with flowers for Candlemas Day

The old Scottish rhyme "If Candlemas Day be fine and clear, there'll be twa winters in the year" explains why February 2 has a divided interest. Mr. Ground Hog shares honor with Candlemas Day. No doubt it is coincidence that the little prophet ground hog, the woodchuck, is lured from his snug winter home on this particular day. But legend has it that if the sun shines brightly so that he sees his shadow, he will hibernate once more, for he knows then that there are six more weeks of cold, cold winter.

As an arranger, you will celebrate in the spirit of Candlemas Day, a throwback to a pagan festival. The burning taper symbolizes the protection of the family from the influence of evil for the balance of the year.

green for St. Patrick's Day
(plates 81, 82)

Just as red is the color of February to symbolize strong emotions—love, passion, patriotism—so is the freshness of green symbolic of March. It is the color of new growth appropriate to the coming of spring after March 21. But as an arranger, green will have another association for you in inspiring your decoration. It is the hue symbolic of the Emerald Isle where a beloved monk, sent from his native land, spread Christianity throughout Ireland. Here he brought a green three-petaled plant (much like our white field clover), using its beautiful tri-symmetry to exemplify the Holy Trinity. Today, this shamrock is Ireland's national emblem, and its color is beloved by all its countrymen. In America, the Irish pay tribute to their revered St. Patrick on his birthday, March 17.

In home decoration, an all-green arrangement would be appropriate. Contrast in texture will contribute intrinsic beauty in the one-hue pattern (Plate 82). For a whimsical note to honor the fun-loving Irish, green leaves grouped around a well-scrubbed potato are amusing. Though originally from America, the Irish grew potatoes easily,

81 (Above Left) SHAMROCK, PIPES, AND IRISH CAPRICE: A *green pottery container with green and white appropriate figurine bust holds white snapdragons, tulips, and anemones with green centers. Ti leaves at the top strengthen silhouette; calla foliage low in the design give weight for balance. Staged against a Kelly-green silk fabric to which a gold-colored shamrock is attached it warms the heart of any one from the Emerald Isle.*
ARRANGER: MRS. F. PALMER HART PHOTOGRAPHER: BOUTRELLE

82 (Above Right) SURE AN' IT'S FROM ERIN YE ARE!: . . . . *when you make an all-green arrangement on March 17. Form and value contrast suggest strength as grand as St. Patrick himself. Materials are white-striped aspidistra leaves (curve these as desired by pulling them gently through thumb and fingers); green Galax leaves (garden ivy would do, too); light green peppers and limes; pale green modern container; stand painted to harmonize.*
ARRANGER: MRS. LOUIS H. AMER PHOTOGRAPHER: CARPENTER'S STUDIO

and when their grain crops failed, they adopted our vegetable as their own. In fact, it was failure of Ireland's potato crop in the middle of the nineteenth century that started the first Irish immigration to the United States.

A *potato* in arrangement! Do I hear a scornful murmur? If so, dear reader, develop that seeing eye. For those who really see, there is "beauty even in common things."

Maypoles and gift baskets for May Day

(plates 83, 84)

Hail to the month of May as she slips in, bringing with her the accessories of spring. The world suddenly becomes new and dazzling. Skies are misty blue, breezes are gentle, the earth is jeweled with flowers, and birds are singing in trees festooned with bloom. All nature is up and doing.

Nothing will make you appreciate Nature and the delightfully different and individual beauty of her four seasons more than planning your arrangements. No one ever indulges in this art without paying homage to Nature. On May Day you will be eager to show evidence

83 IN THANKFUL JOY BECAUSE THE SPRING IS HERE: *About a beautifully sculptured bronze girl with gracefully flowing garment, a rhythmic branch of Norway maple, twigs tipped with its delicate chartreuse flowers, two varieties of yellow narcissus, green and white hosta leaves, and lush green foliage from the moisture loving skunk cabbage convey an outward expression of man's common heritage of joy on May Day which honors one of the oldest festivals transplanted from British soil.*

ARRANGER: MRS. RAYMOND R. STOLTZ PHOTOGRAPHER: BOUTRELLE

84 THIS MAY DAY ARRANGEMENT: . . . *would surely erase all sorrow and sadness from the house. On bark peeled from a birch tree, a little calf seems awed by the arrangement of tulip tree branches, iris bloom, and intriguing "calves' tongue" foliage. Dried disks of lunaria are included to echo the white on the accessory calf. All is in brown, yellow, white with a touch of green.*

ARRANGER: MRS. SAMUEL LASKER PHOTOGRAPHER: BOUTRELLE

of the yearly miracle of renewal. You will enjoy "bringing in the May" as people did in ancient times when, on May 1, Romans celebrated the festival "Floralia" in honor of Flora, goddess of blooming vegetation. Games and dancing to express joy at the return of spring began in the Orient, swept to Greece and Rome, and then to other parts of the European continent. Among the various customs throughout the world, perhaps those of the Maypole and May basket have been most popular.

In England, a tall, straight tree was carried to the location of celebration by oxen whose horns were decorated with flowery garlands. Stripped of branches and wound with ribbon, the tree was set up in readiness for the dance. The sight of young people, each holding a ribbon as they dance around a Maypole in revival of this ancient custom is an impressive one, and an inspiration for your decoration.

I have fond recollections of hanging a small homemade paper basket filled with violets, still wet with early morning moisture, on the doorknob of my mother's bedroom for a surprise on May Day. The memory of the joy it brought has lingered long.

Some years back, a May gift basket was hung on my own front door by a friend who has unusual insight. Nested among young, crinkly, chartreuse-hued leaves of rhubarb and uncurling fronds of a woodland fern was a small square basket of meadow bluets to be planted later in my rockery. My childhood delight in seeing Pennsylvania fields each spring, echoing the color of the heavens in their thick matting of dainty "Quaker ladies", came back to me with this basket, a touching tribute to be cherished in memory always.

The sight of a basket filled with flowers of May hanging from the knocker on the front door of any home is quaint and heartwarming and well worth the time and trouble you may take to revive this old-time practice.

novelty decorations for intimate days

Everyone loves celebrations, so do not lose any opportunity to decorate for the affair. In addition to the popular holidays and festive days discussed, you will enjoy making plans for any number of "intimate" days—days that hold a personal meaning and happiness for family and friends.

85 FOR A NOVEMBER BIRTHDAY: *An original and exquisite example of decoration inspired by the November child's flower, chrysanthemum, and the yellow of her birthstone, topaz. It might well honor the birthday of any family member or intimate friend born in the year's 11th month. Oriental influence is shown, and appropriately so, for the Chinese, more than any other people, appreciate the flower for its symbolism of integrity and courage.*

ARRANGER: MRS. JOHN W. KNIGHT, JR. PHOTOGRAPHER: DWITE WALKER

86 "AND THERE SHALL BE SIGNS IN SUN AND MOON AND STARS"* : A *birthday arrangement in honor of one born under the royal sign of the Zodiac, Leo the Lion. According to astrology, those born between July 23 and August 24 are masterful individuals. One has but to glance at this design of strong forceful tropical materials to see decoration that is congenial to Leo-born sons and daughters. Yellow-green birds nest fern with red-brown edging and center markings tie in with copper-red stems and backs of species begonia leaves used for depth and transition. With deep green perforated leaves of monstera climber at the focal area, they complement a black ceramic lion.*

ARRANGER: MRS. JOHN B. DUNNING PHOTOGRAPHER: BOUTRELLE

* St. Luke, XXI, 25.

Birthdays in particular should be joyous occasions. They are the most individual celebrations and, for that reason, the most challenging. There will be unique hobbies and experiences to serve as decorative inspiration, each different from those of others. Then too, each month has its symbolic stone and flower (Plate 85), and its astrological sign of the zodiac. People respond happily to novelty decoration if it is used within the bounds of good taste. It can be quite expressive of a definite mood; often the spirit is that of amusement.

Children, particularly, enjoy humorous, story-telling compositions. There is a place for humor in all art, and if one cannot be as a child on occasion, life has lost its thrill! The flower-show design in Plate 88 is a mirth-provoking illustration. It is not difficult to appreciate such a setting staged in a whoopee party room, in honor of dad on his birthday.

87 TO THE BRIDE: *Traditionally trimmed with symbols reminiscent of every wedding, lace, frills, flowers, and thrills combine beautifully to produce a wedding table lovely as an exquisite painting. It is a setting guaranteed to go far toward making a wedding reception one to be long remembered.*
ARRANGER: MRS. DAVID KIRSCHENBAUM PHOTOGRAPHER: BOUTRELLE

parties for the bride and groom
(plates 87, 88)

A party for a bride can be simple, but festive and sentimentally feminine, worked out perhaps in cool pale blues, or delicate greens and yellows, or youthful pinks, and inspiring white. The happy news can be announced at a breakfast party, a luncheon, a dinner, or a delightful interlude at teatime.

When the bride-to-be entertains her bridesmaids and matron of honor, no one else is present, so the charm of intimacy should prevail in decoration.

The masculine version of this traditional affair is the bachelor party given by the groom for his ushers and most intimate friends a night or two before the wedding. Suitable decorations will favor the masculine taste for bold and decisive pattern.

88 BACHELOR'S PARTY: *Titled "Cloudy and Overcast" and complete in amusing detail, this whoopee-room decoration supplies merriment on* his *traditional "last night of freedom". Except to call attention to the free-hand, charcoal drawn background, no description can do justice to this hilarious bit of make believe.*
ARRANGER: MRS. SIMEON TAYLOR SHIELDS PHOTOGRAPHER: DORN'S PHOTO SHOP

the wedding decorations
(plate 87)

To crown the exciting day, the wedding table may be planned for breakfast, luncheon, or an afternoon or evening reception. It will be as lovely as an exquisite painting, in white as tradition dictates, or in the delicate pastels that have recently been accepted. In either case, fresh, crisp and gay should be the adjectives for the less formal, pomp and splendor for the more formal tables.

There is nothing nicer for the centerpiece than the traditional bride's cake, the triumph of the baker's art, ornamented with flowers and topped with a suitable motif—bell, dove, or bridal pair. An intriguing custom from Bermuda is worth mentioning. The cake is topped with a tiny evergreen tree. The roots are kept fresh with dampened sphagnum moss, carefully and neatly wrapped with metal-foil paper. Just before the happy bride with her husband, in traditional manner, cuts the first serving of cake, the tree is removed, to be planted later as a symbol of hope by the newlyweds.

There is no substitute for flowers to enhance the home as setting for the marriage ceremony. It should be gay with decorations, simple and seemingly spontaneous. Remember, accent is on the bride! Stock and gladiolus, carnations and gardenias in unrelieved green and white, go far to add to the beauty of this solemn but joyous occasion. The satin loveliness of white roses in sparkling crystal or dainty sweet-peas enhanced by bright green leaves lend calm and charm to the ceremony that takes place in the home.

wedding anniversaries can be versatile
(plates 89, 90)

As time moves on, yearly anniversaries come jogging along in a couple's life. When they have reached their fiftieth year together, the anniversary event is unique and a must for celebration! A golden yellow scheme would symbolize "the golden sunshine of life," and the heart remembers. Time looked back on seems such a little while.

But each wedded year brings its special day. Recently, I was guest at a tenth or tin anniversary party breakfast. The accessories were tin, of the kitchen-utensil variety. Its shiny surface and form in modern and good design played second only to the imagination displayed by the hostess.

89 ARRANGEMENT FOR AN ANNIVERSARY: *Roses, Good News variety, deep to pale coral in color, with their foliage, and copper-hued beech, the new growth lightening to coral, proclaim the modern touch in this antique bisque vase with brown and coral ornamentation and gilded handles. A lace-trimmed wedding fan and lace hankie pulled through the handle complete the picture.*
ARRANGER: MRS. RAYMOND R. STOLTZ PHOTOGRAPHER: BOUTRELLE

90 GOLDEN WEDDING: *Fifty years in the life of a happy couple appropriately told by a story in gold. Aspidistra, magnolia, wheat, rice, artichokes and pine cones are gilded by hand and arranged in exquisitely etched containers of gleaming brass. The symbolic rings are wrapped neatly with ribbon of gold satin—all is truly a golden dividend.*

ARRANGER: MRS. THOMAS STEED PHOTOGRAPHER: OFFIE LITES

At one end of the table, on a red and white checked cloth, a round cake tin was placed on a larger square tin in epergne effect. It held red and white geraniums accented with big shiny leaves of ivy. The design was clean-cut and crisp in a style suited to metal. The table was skilfully balanced with a grouping of red and white stub candles at the opposite end. White pottery dishes, red coarse-weave napkins, and a most gala mood completed this engaging table.

special occasions inspire definite styles

In a book such as this something planned to greet the sick on any special day is worth consideration. One who is bedridden finds importance in the little things, so flowers wisely chosen and designed with respect for his color and texture preferences, his special interest (as the unusual container in plate 104), and his well being, make a penned-in world more interesting.

Avoid short-lived bloom, highly-scented varieties, and strong, harsh color. Gay clear tones and pastels are excellent, for they will not tire his eyes. Make the arrangement at home, securing the plant material in place with a well anchored stem holder (a pin type is useful in a flat container; chicken wire crumpled and placed inside the vase serves well when the receptacle is tall). The completed composition is carried to the shut-in in a corrugated box. Stuff newspapers into the corners to prevent the arrangement from shifting position to endanger the design.

Of novelty decorations, those planned as a toast to a "bon voyage" can be fun to do. Even if you have never visited the world's corner that is luring your honor guest or guests, you need not concern yourself with realities. Give free rein to your imagination in interpreting the characteristics of the intended destination (Plates 98, 99, 100).

There is the party for the sweet girl graduate, when casual simplicity is in order. There is the day when the subdeb invites her crowd to food and fun galore—no "silly fluff" arrangements for her. There is Arbor Day, when you entertain your garden club after a tree-planting ceremony. Or April 23, Shakespeare's birthday, when you decorate for a literary club around the theme of "All the world's a stage". And so it goes, many and varied occasions to influence beautiful, inspiring, and appropriate decorative arrangements.

Suggestions for some of the many special occasions to inspire a definite style or type of decoration are pictured in *Holiday Flower Arrangements.*

The very nicest thing about this whole idea of decorating the home for holidays and personal occasions is that the possibilities are endless. As the year progresses, there are fresh themes to please and stimulate designer and spectator alike. "There is no limit," said a professor of horticulture, "to the production of crops on the mental soil."

91 FOR THE SWEET GIRL GRADUATE: *Delicate hues in flowers are combined with dainty foliage in effective decoration on a luncheon table set for a young girl's graduation party. The horizontal flair in the floral grouping is particularly inviting in the high container such as this crystal compote. Such fragile and feminine beauty would be appropriate at a wedding celebration, on the announcement table, or to lend atmosphere at the party planned for sweet sixteen.*
ARRANGER: MRS. GEORGE J. HIRSCH PHOTOGRAPHER: BOUTRELLE

This wisdom is applicable here. Bring together definite color plans, favored textures, beautiful containers, appropriate accessories, and imaginative ideas for drama, charm, and fun. Let your work be dignified, casual, daring, quaint, sentimental, anything you wish, but above all, let your decorations for special occasions be personal. Design is born of the imagination. Unless you animate your arrangements with your own personality, you will have neither success nor fun!

92 (Left) CHILDRENS' DAY TOKEN: *In many church in America the second Sunday in June is designated as Chi dren's Day. Perhaps this lovely custom grew from our Savior words, "Suffer little children to come unto me and forbid the not, for such is the kingdom of heaven".* White *carnations a appropriate for their symbolism in the language of flowers: "I' never forget". Other unsophisticated flowers would serve well—the casual daisy for example, symbol of innocence.*
ARRANGER: MRS. RAYMOND R. STOLTZ PHOTOGRAPHER: BO TRELLE

93 (Below) AT THE CHARITY BENEFIT: A *money tre is easy to make, practical, and is sure to inspire those who atten the affair to remember its purpose! Make it on a flat wire mes foundation wedged into a flower pot painted in harmonizin green. See page 38 for directions on covering such a frame.* Wir *together gold foil-covered make believe coins (inexpensive foi wrapped candy coins are easy to attach). Allow sufficient wir to fasten the clusters onto the foundation of greens. Occasion harmonizing or contrasting satin bows add variety and texture*
ARRANGER: MRS. LOUIS H. AMER PHOTOGRAPHER: EDWARD I MAHER

94 (Above) BACK TO SCHOOL WITH AN APPLE FOR TEACHER: *Depicting an occasion typical of autumn this sporting composition is a salute to the girl or boy off to school. Red geraniums in a wooden tub are positioned on a worn seat from a child's maple wagon. An old McGuffey's reader and a bright, shiny red apple are accessories. Background is pumpkin color in an all over calico patterned design.*

ARRANGER: MRS. WENDELL KILMER PHOTOGRAPHER: BOUTRELLE

95 (Right) THE NIGHT OF THE BIG FIGHT: *Red-orange chrysanthemums, orange-berried shrub, and peony foliage that has donned its autumnal brown-red cloak are arranged in a boxer's glove, its mate an accessory. Such novelty assures stimulation at the T.V. party scheduled on the night of the big fight.*

ARRANGER: MRS. GERSON T. HIRSCH PHOTOGRAPHER: BOUTRELLE

96 (Opposite Above) THE RED SHOES: *For a party after the theater, ballet figures in tones of red to pink, with roses, chrysanthemums, and carnations in similar hues, and gray-green foliage, are combined in a honey-colored alabaster container.*

ARRANGER: MRS. JAMES L. FINCH PHOTOGRAPHER: BOUTRELLE

97 (Opposite Below) FOR A PARTY AFTER WINTER SPORTS: *This eleven-year-old arranger is truly creative in this original piece. White gladiolus with white chrysanthemums as transition between these spikes and the skates, unlike in form or substance.*

ARRANGER: JOANN BLUMBERG (AGE 11 YEARS) PHOTOGRAPHER: BOUTRELLE

98 (Below) TOAST TO THE TRAVELER: *A send-off buffet to the traveler bound for lazy vacation days on sea-washed shores, this setting employs a conch shell in creamy tan and pink, staged on a piece of weathered driftwood. Echeveria blossoms and foliage rosettes in mauve and green-blue tones, pink snapdragons, and lupine seed pods of blue-green are combined to achieve an impression of motion.*

ARRANGER: MRS. H. HENRY STALEY PHOTOGRAPHER: BOUTRELLE

99 & 100 FAREWELL TO THE SOUTH SEA ISLANDS: *The two views of one luncheon table decoration are best described in the arranger's own words: "An exotic sculptured head, softened by chartreuse Fugi chrysanthemums beckons across rolling waves of ti leaves. Reverse side of arrangement depicts lush growth of islands and incorporates peppers, avocados, cucumber 'water lilies', green grapes, and variegated philodendron. The black plastic base picks up the texture and color of the head, as well as tying arrangement to monk's cloth table covering." This work is excellent for a table piece because there is a variety of pattern seen from all angles.*

ARRANGER: MRS. HOWARD S. KITTEL PHOTOGRAPHER: ANTHONY STOKER

101 VACATION MEMORIES: *A rippled pattern on a hand-carved board represents the water's edge. Grasses follow the curve of the neck of the ceramic duck. Bearded wheat, durum and einkorn wheat, cattails, pampas grass, a wood stump, and wood moss form rhythmic design to convey vacation memories.*
ARRANGER: MRS. SAMUEL LASKER PHOTOGRAPHER: BOUTRELLE

102 BERMUDA BEAUTY: *On a large teakwood base, white gardenias and their lovely refined foliage are arranged in and around a magnificent piece of white coral obtained on that "one long holiday". Variegated leaves in green and white, and three white orchids complete a stunning grouping to induce a mood of remembering.*

ARRANGER: MRS. THOMAS STEED PHOTOGRAPHER: OFFIE LITES

103 PEACE OFFERING TO WINTER: *For a gathering of garden club enthusiasts, this story-telling composition would be particularly appropriate. It is composed with Southern pine and red nandina berries in an antique green pottery bowl.*

ARRANGER: MRS. EDGAR LITTMANN PHOTOGRAPHER: CHARLES TREFTS

104 CHEER FOR THE SHUT-IN: *A gift of this wrought-iron lantern alight with sunny-yellow, long-lasting chrysanthemums, would gladden the sick-abed arranger's heart, not only for its beauty, but because it will add a unique container to her collection.*

ARRANGER: MRS. JAMES L. FINCH PHOTOGRAPHER: BOUTRELLE

Lists for Special Occasions

CALENDAR OF HOLIDAYS GENERALLY OBSERVED

JANUARY
1 New Year's Day

FEBRUARY
2 Candlemas and Ground hog Days
14 Valentine Day
12 Lincoln's Birthday
22 Washington's Birthday

MARCH
17 Saint Patrick's Day
Easter a Sunday in the 35 day period between March 21 through April 25

APRIL
Easter may fall on a Sunday prior to April 26
1 April Fools' Day (no special decoration called for)
6 Army Day

MAY
1 May Day
13 Indian Day (in most states)
Mother's Day 2nd Sunday
30 Memorial Day (originally called "Decoration Day")

JUNE
14 Flag Day
Children's Day (observed in many churches) 2nd Sunday
Father's Day 3rd Sunday

JULY
4 Independence Day

SEPTEMBER
Labor Day 1st Monday

OCTOBER
12 Columbus Day
27 Navy Day
31 Halloween

NOVEMBER
1 All Saints' Day
11 Armistice Day
Thanksgiving 4th Thursday

DECEMBER
25 Christmas

WEDDING ANNIVERSARIES

FIRST	Paper	THIRTEENTH	Lace
SECOND	Cotton	FOURTEENTH	Ivory
THIRD	Leather	FIFTEENTH	Crystal
FOURTH	Books or Fruits & Flowers	TWENTIETH	China
FIFTH	Wooden	TWENTY-FIFTH	Silver
SIXTH	Iron or Sugar & Candy	THIRTIETH	Pearl
SEVENTH	Woolen or Copper	THIRTY-FIFTH	Coral
EIGHTH	Rubber or Bronze	FORTIETH	Ruby
NINTH	Pottery or Willow	FORTY-FIFTH	Sapphire
TENTH	Aluminum and Tin	FIFTIETH	Golden
ELEVENTH	Steel	FIFTY-FIFTH	Emerald
TWELFTH	Silk and Linen	SEVENTY-FIFTH	Diamond

SYMBOLIC FLOWERS AND BIRTHSTONES

MONTH	FLOWER	STONE
January	Carnation	Garnet
February	Violet	Amethyst
March	Jonquil	Aquamarine; Bloodstone
April	Sweet Pea	Diamond
May	Lily of the Valley	Emerald
June	Rose	Pearl; Moonstone; alexandrite
July	Larkspur	Ruby
August	Gladiolus	Peridot; sardonyx
September	Aster	Sapphire
October	Calendula	Opal; Tourmaline
November	Chrysanthemum	Topaz
December	Narcissus	Turquoise; Zircon; Lapis-lazuli

SIGNS OF THE ZODIAC

SIGN	SYMBOL	DATE		
first	Aries (Ram)	March 22	through	April 20
second	Taurus (Bull)	April 21	"	May 21
third	Gemini (Twins)	May 22	"	June 21
fourth	Cancer (Crab)	June 22	"	July 23
fifth	Leo (Lion)	July 24	"	August 23
sixth	Virgo (Virgin)	August 24	"	Sept. 23
seventh	Libra (Scales)	Sept. 24	"	Oct. 23
eighth	Scorpio (Scorpion)	Oct. 24	"	Nov. 22
ninth	Sagittarius (Man with arrow)	Nov. 23	"	Dec. 22
tenth	Capricorn (Goat)	Dec. 23	"	Jan. 20
eleventh	Aquarius (Man pouring water)	Jan. 21	"	Feb. 19
twelfth	Pisces (Two fishes swimming in opposite directions)	Feb. 20	"	March 21

STATE FLOWERS

State	Flower
ALABAMA	Goldenrod
ARIZONA	Giant Cactus
ARKANSAS	Apple Blossom
CALIFORNIA	Golden Poppy
COLORADO	Columbine
CONNECTICUT	Mountain Laurel
DELAWARE	Peach Blossom
DISTRICT OF COLUMBIA	American Beauty Rose
FLORIDA	Orange Blossom
GEORGIA	Cherokee Rose
IDAHO	Syringa
ILLINOIS	Violet
INDIANA	Zinnia
IOWA	Wild Rose
KANSAS	Sunflower
KENTUCKY	Goldenrod
LOUISIANA	Magnolia
MAINE	Pine Cone and Tassel
MARYLAND	Blackeyed Susan
MASSACHUSETTS	Arbutus (May Flower)
MICHIGAN	Apple Blossom
MINNESOTA	Moccasin Flower
MISSISSIPPI	Magnolia
MISSOURI	Hawthorn
MONTANA	Bitter Root
NEBRASKA	Goldenrod
NEVADA	Sagebush
NEW HAMPSHIRE	Purple Lilac
NEW JERSEY	Violet
NEW MEXICO	Yucca
NEW YORK	Rose
NORTH CAROLINA	Daisy
NORTH DAKOTA	Wild Prairie Rose
OHIO	Scarlet Carnation
OKLAHOMA	Mistletoe
OREGON	Oregon Grape
PENNSYLVANIA	Mountain Laurel
RHODE ISLAND	Violet
SOUTH CAROLINA	YellowJessamine
SOUTH DAKOTA	Pasque Flower
TENNESSEE	Iris
TEXAS	Bluebonnet
UTAH	Sego Lily
VERMONT	Red Clover
VIRGINIA	Dogwood
WASHINGTON	Rhododendron
WEST VIRGINIA	Rhododendron
WISCONSIN	Violet
WYOMING	Indian Paintbrush
HAWAII	Hibiscus
ALASKA	Forget-Me-Not

LANGUAGE OF FLOWERS

(compiled by Society of American Florists, chartered by act of Congress)

BLUE VIOLETS *I'll be true, always*
PINK CARNATION *I'll never forget you*
CHRYSANTHEMUM *You're a wonderful friend*
GARDENIA *You're lovely*
IRIS *Your friendship means much to me*
ORCHID *Beautiful lady*
PANSIES *Thinking of you*
PURPLE HYACINTH *Forgive me*
RED ROSE *I love you*
SWEET PEAS *Thank you for a lovely time*
WHITE ROSE *You're heavenly*
YELLOW TULIP *There's sunshine in your smile*

Index